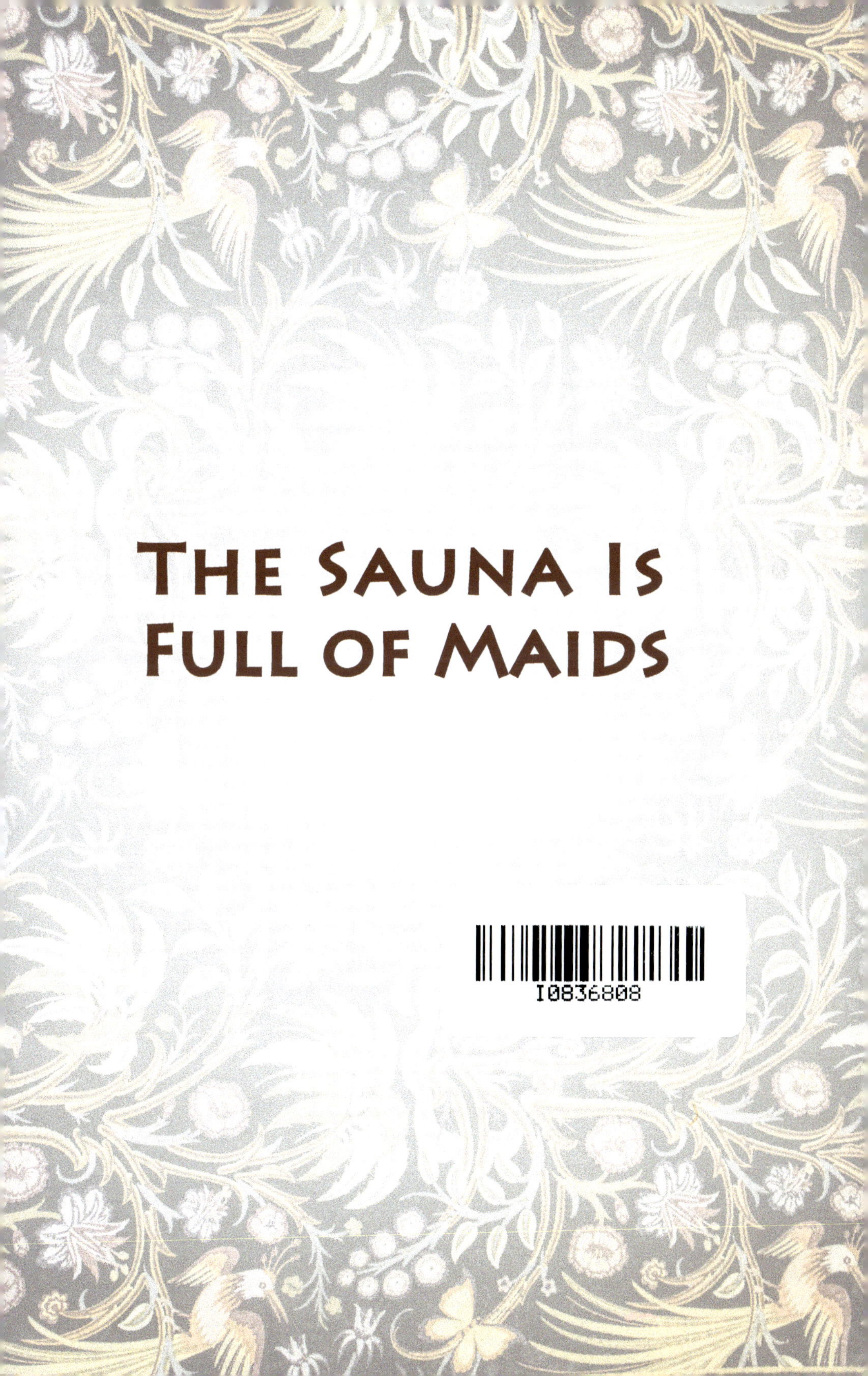
THE SAUNA IS
FULL OF MAIDS
I0836808

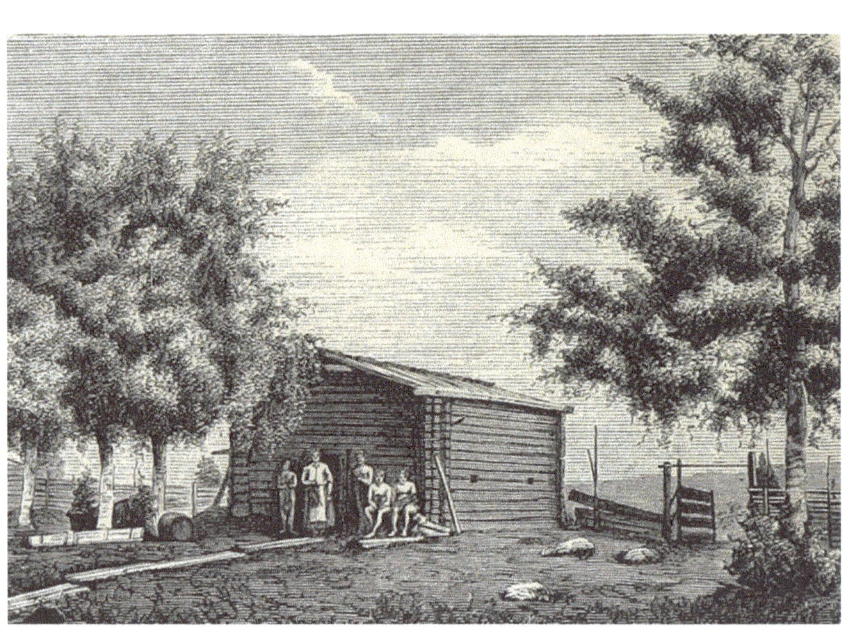

The Sauna Is Full of Maids

poems by

Cheryl J. Fish

Shanti Arts Publishing

Brunswick, Maine 04011

The Sauna Is Full of Maids

Published by Shanti Arts Publishing
Interior and cover design by Shanti Arts Designs

Background design on cover and page 1 by
ThomasW01. Wikimedia Commons. Creative Commons
Attribution-Share Alike 4.0 International license.

Shanti Arts LLC
193 Hillside Road
Brunswick, Maine 04011
shantiarts.com

Printed in the United States of America

ISBN: 978-1-951651-74-9 (softcover)

Library of Congress Control Number: 2021936154

And the hare ran off . . .
To the sauna threshold it ran,
on the threshold it squats
the sauna is full of maids;
whisks in hand they greet. . .

— from the *Kalevala, Book 4*;
390–461 (Finnish National Epic)

Contents

Preface

Now that Finnish sauna culture has been added to UNESCO's Representative List of the Intangible Cultural Heritage of Humanity, I am proud to have long recognized and celebrated *lingua sauna* as a tangible and sublime experience. As I write this, the COVID-19 pandemic has passed its first-year anniversary, so the opportunities that enabled this book seem ever more precious. These poems were inspired most of all by friendship; I am filled with gratitude for thirteen years of experiences in saunas, lakes, villages, homes, Siida, streets, and parks of Finland (with some visits to Sweden and Norway too) since I first spent a semester as Fulbright professor of North American Studies at University of Tampere in 2007. I was accompanied by my son Joshua who was seven going on eight, and he went to second grade in Tampere.

My many returns to Finland were to expand my research on protest and resistance to mining and extraction in Arctic Fennoscandia in the works of Sami filmmakers, photographers, and artists. This relates to my earlier writing on identity and resistance in multi-ethnic American, feminist, and environmental justice approaches to literature, film, and architecture. However, the landscapes and experiences evoked poetry and rich stories. For the works in this collection, I found influence in rhythms and characters of the Finnish national epic poem, the *Kalevala,* Elias Lönnrot's compilation of oral folklore and mythology, originally published in 1835. My reading of the epic is based on the English translation by Keith Bosley, published by Oxford University Press. In my research on Sami art and film, as well as attendance at the Riddu-Riddu international indigenous festival, cultural centers, universities, and museums, I learned about various forms of Sami resistance, spiritual expression, and resiliency. I am grateful for the connections that enabled and heightened many of these experiences.

Sami artists, scholars, and friends shared family traditions, histories, and the traumatic outcomes of settler-colonialism in

Sápmi, which demonized and erased Sami culture and continues to do so. I appreciate the time, openness, and access I was granted. It deeply resonated and connected with my sense of the brutal treatment of Native Americans and African Americans in the U.S. My maternal grandmother was her family's sole survivor during the Holocaust. These factors influence my scholarship and teaching to advocate for Sami sovereignty and indigenous rights. It's necessary to acknowledge different cultural histories and unequal access by the Sami to rights and governance in the Nordic nations.

I wish to acknowledge the importance of Tim Frandy's recent translations into English of Inari Sami *yoiks* and the cultural work they perform, and Rauna Kuokkanen's feminist writings on gender, human rights, and Sami subjectivities. In these poems, I mix actual references with poetic license to blend, blur, concoct, and dream. Notes on the photographic images are provided at the end of this book.

Acknowledgments

The author would like to thank the editors of the following journals where these poems first appeared, sometimes in slightly different versions:

Hanging Loose 109, 2018: "Gulf of Finland";
New American Writing 36, 2018: "The Thin Man at Kuusijärvi Sauna" and "Flesh from Stone";
Postcard Poems, March 23, 2019: "Prior Previous-ness," [https://postcardpoemsandprose.wordpress.com/2019/03/22/prior-previousness-by-cheryl-fish];
Poetics for the More-than-Human World (anthology), edited by Mary Newell, Bernard Quetchenbach, and Sarah Nolan: "Artist's Residency at Ii, Finland," "The Ice Hotel at Jukkasjärvi, Sweden," and "Unreliable Snowpack"; appeared in the online, and also in print, Dispatches Editions, Spuyten Duyvil Press, 2021.

Thanks to the staff and founders of the KulttuuriKauppila residency in Ii, Finland, an inspiration and locale where some of these poems and photographs originated during a month-long residence. Also the Kulttuuritalo Päiväkoti residence on Hailuoto Island where I spent an inspiring overnight visit. "Flesh from Stone" was turned into a song composed by Katie Bishop. Thanks to the Fulbright Finland staff, especially Suzanne Louis, Emilia Holopainen, and Terhi Molsa, for support and for promoting educational exchanges between Americans and Finns. Some travel for research and writing was funded in part by grants from the PSC-CUNY Research Foundation. I benefited from a Seed Box short-term research grant in environmental humanities, supported with funding from Mistra and Formas, at Linköping University in Sweden. Residences at Drop, Forge and Tool, and Wellspring House provided quiet time in which to write. Michelle M. Tokarczyk, Sri Lal, Eileen P. Kennedy, and Ellen Rittenberg offered feedback on some of these poems-in-progress. Thanks to the Finland Center in New York City for the opportunity to read some of these poems at the Finland100 Street Fair in 2017, and to Angie Pohja for arranging a poetry reading and musical afternoon with her band at the Gobi Desert Canoe Club in Tampere in 2018. Thanks to Christine Cote at Shanti Arts for making this collection possible.

I am indebted to the following persons for exchanges that included one or more of the following: sharing sauna rituals, Sami traditions, family history, hospitality, companionship/ conversation, and research that inspired these poems and photos: Lena Stenberg, Liselotte Wajstedt, Mikael Johansson, Kaisa Huuva, Ellacarin Blind, Annika Lindman, Angie and Tommi Pohja, Jussi Hirvi, Sanna Koivisto, Sanna Roukala, Antti Leinonen, Päivi Kuoppala, Aniqa and Tanveer Sandhu, Toni Lahtinen, Maria Laakaso, Carola Grahn, Marja Helander, Pekka Makkonen, Mikku Saiku, Markku Henriksson, Lea Backman, Dave Sponde, Markus Kaitila, Marko Jouste, Mina Halonen, Heini Perttula, Veikko Renkonen, Julian Renkonen, Anni-Sofia Kauppila, Terry Carter, Tom Manwell, Karen Matthews, Jane Weiss, Toni Simon, Marjorie Shaffer, Michael Hurd, Iris Tukiainen, Pirjo Virtanen, Hanna Guttorm, and Lea Kantonen.

All references to the *Kalevala* are from the Oxford edition in English translated by Keith Bosley.

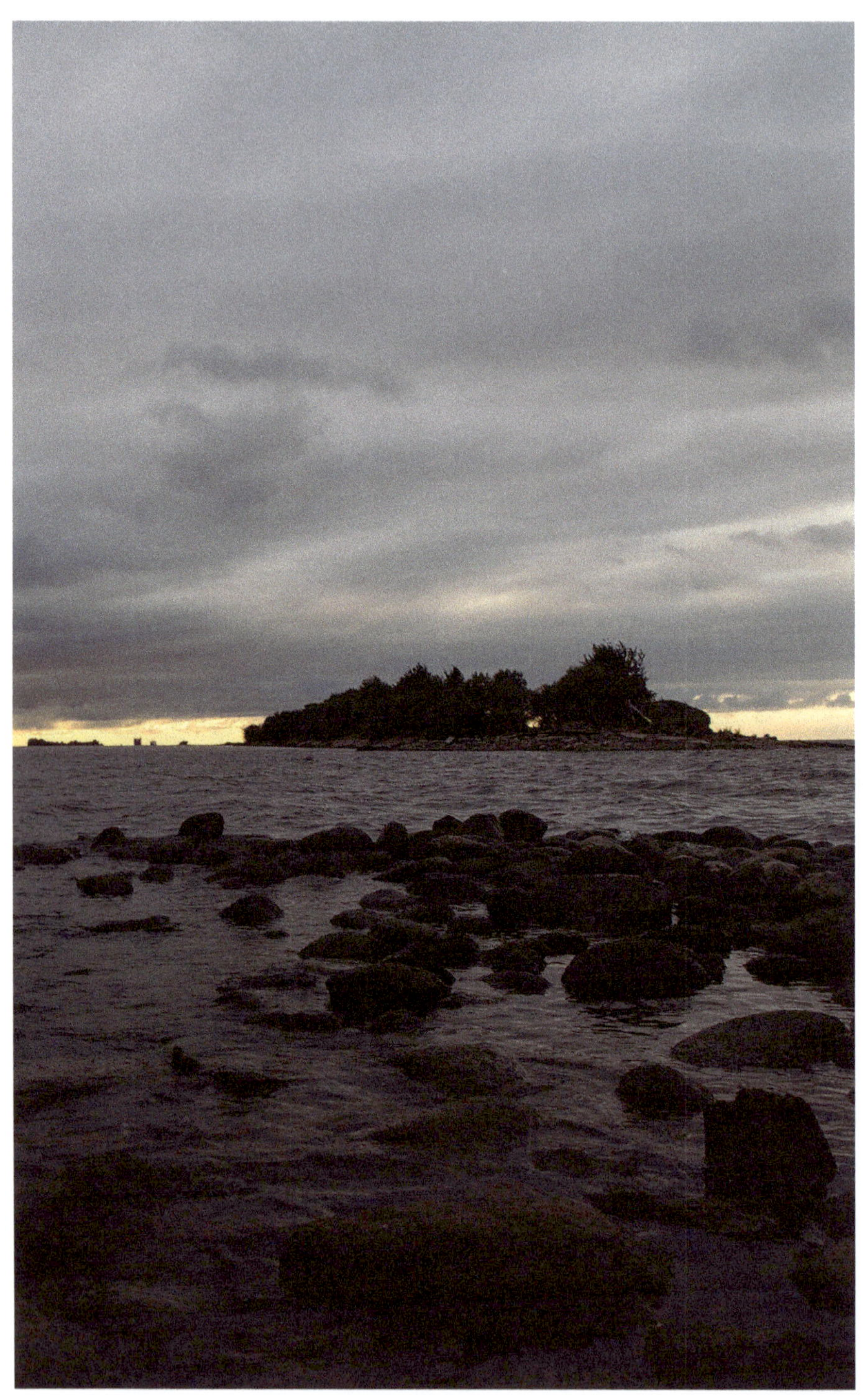

Gulf of Finland

for Angie Pohja

Can I use my miles to get more miles?
They never expire. Flea market to closet.
A calm naked swim in Yrjönkatu simhall, then smoke sauna.

Have a Lapin Kulta Premium. Find out who's where.

Angie's singing. She sways and scat sings, the guitar rolls.
She's on stage in the crowded bar.

Go and hit the water. Swim naked, then sit
        in the smoke sauna
hot on a wood bench, top row. Out into cold pool.

Annika shows me where they wash rugs with a brush
        in the Gulf of Finland.
After a pounding, they hang from the rug dock. Long periods of light.

Lena tells me of churlish reindeer having their ears marked.
Slaughter in autumn.

Viili is a dairy product that tastes like glue; *piimä* quiet buttermilk
        on tongue.

Angie's an American married to a Finn who works nights.
She sings and sways in the pubs and halls of Tampere.

Like Väinämöinen in the *Kalevala*.
Hot molten blues in foam and beer.

Oh Lake Näsijärvi.

Songs Captivate the Traveler

Could it be a sha-man, or sha-woman blows through this
wind and water? *Joik*; poetry; exoneration. Songs captivate
the traveler. Human-animal-stone-tree. A ritual for warm hands.
We tried to find my spirit guide in her Brooklyn apartment.
Is it a turtle, a rabbit, a magpie? We don't know.
The Hebrew word for soul, *nephesh,* denotes all animal life.

Poems begin and end as songs. How can the cuckoo bless a forest
if only one tree remains unfelled?
I dwell in the Northland for inspired intervals. Lapland. Ostrobothnia.
Helsinki. Troms-Finnmark. Tampere.
I apologize for my Americanness.
The sound of my voice interferes with sky shapes.
Impatient with what separates us. Meet me again soon.
Silence. River, I miss your shadows.

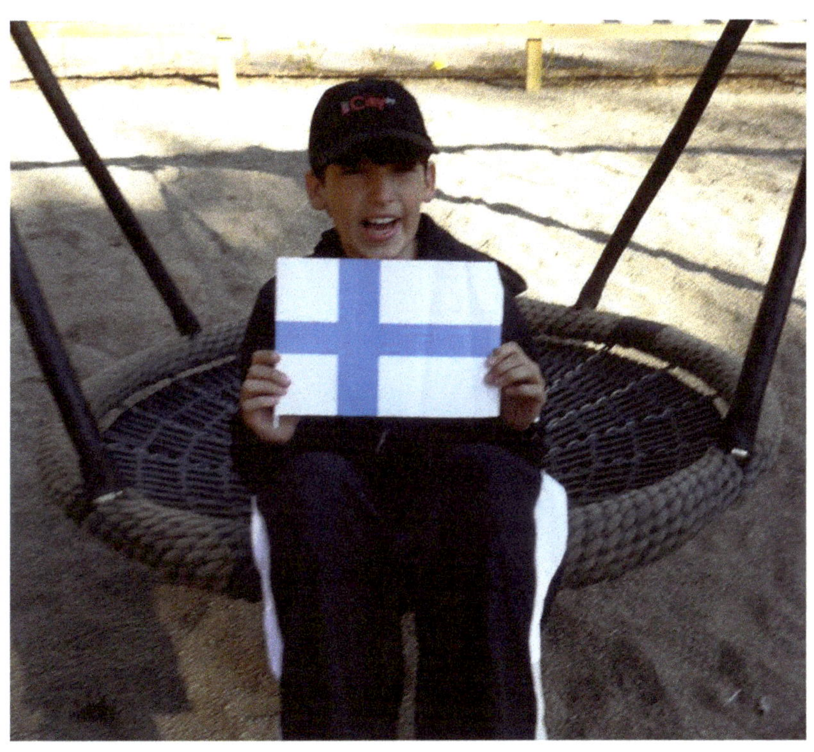

The Thin Man at Kuusijärvi Sauna

for Jussi

The thin man wearing a cap at the Kuusijärvi smoke sauna
makes it hot enough
to melt a stone. When he throws water steam hisses
in the small wooden room.
Lips sear off my face.
He cultivates heat like wanton love.

His sampo, his compass, molding the pyre itself.
Sing your song backwards!
The smoke flew up the flue
while we ate reindeer meat and lingonberry.
Smoke curved in wisps
Then it shot from the walls and chimney.

Fire fighters came to unfurl their hoses.
We watched them spray and shout water
And the thin man for whom heat is a favorite toy
Walked out immaculate.

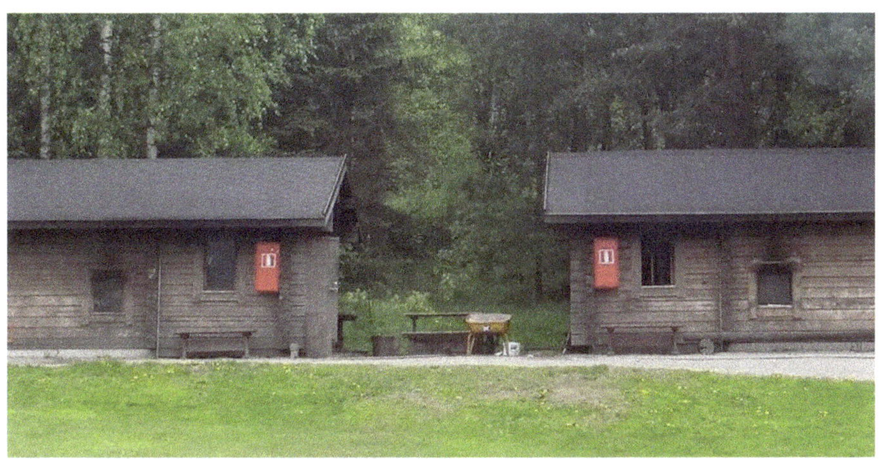

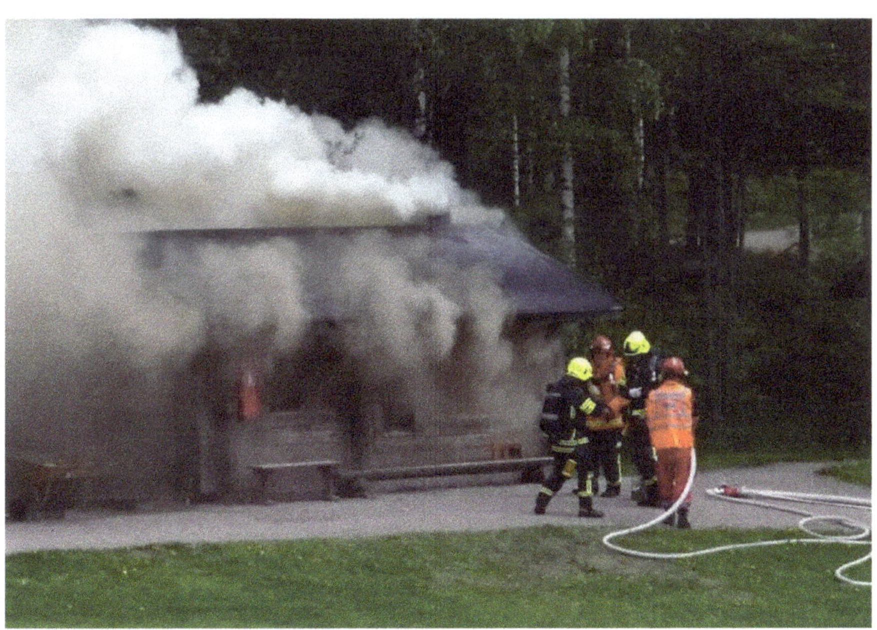

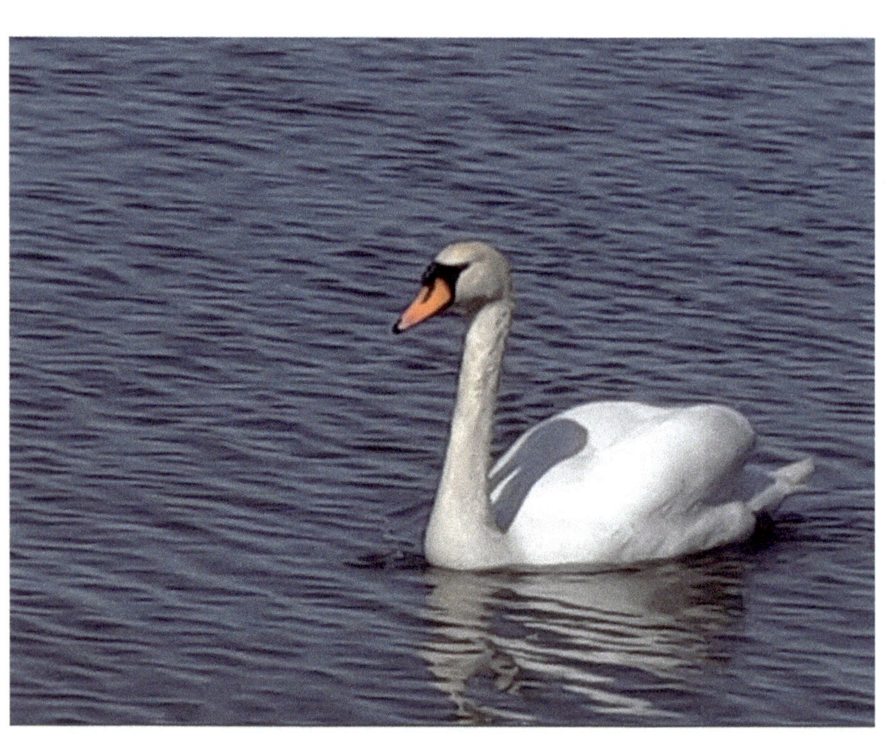

Flesh from Stone

Jessop tells me he slept with that slim married woman he spots in the cafe in Kallio. She's sharing a salad and some fish with her husband. We do not stay. It would be too awkward. The urge to fuck her has passed. Even though he identifies as gay, Jessop was drawn to her glow, cat mixed with witch. The sensual arts can't be explained. Later, Jessop takes me to the bar near the water where he meets men he takes home. He cannot imagine loving them longer than a midnight sun's worth of calories. I have been alone. Unable to connect dashes and dots, find magnetic friction. In Helsinki, I see statues of water nymphs, beautiful marble bodies, and magpies sounding like American crows. Jessop experiences chemical sensitivity, electromagnetic allergies, feels the pull of night-time jazz. He takes me to the saunas: the large one by the Olympic Stadium, the smoke sauna outside the city with a lunch buffet. We talk and sweat, then drink beer. The city unfolds in the present of presence, melding steam from green. Sex between solitude, separating flesh from stone.

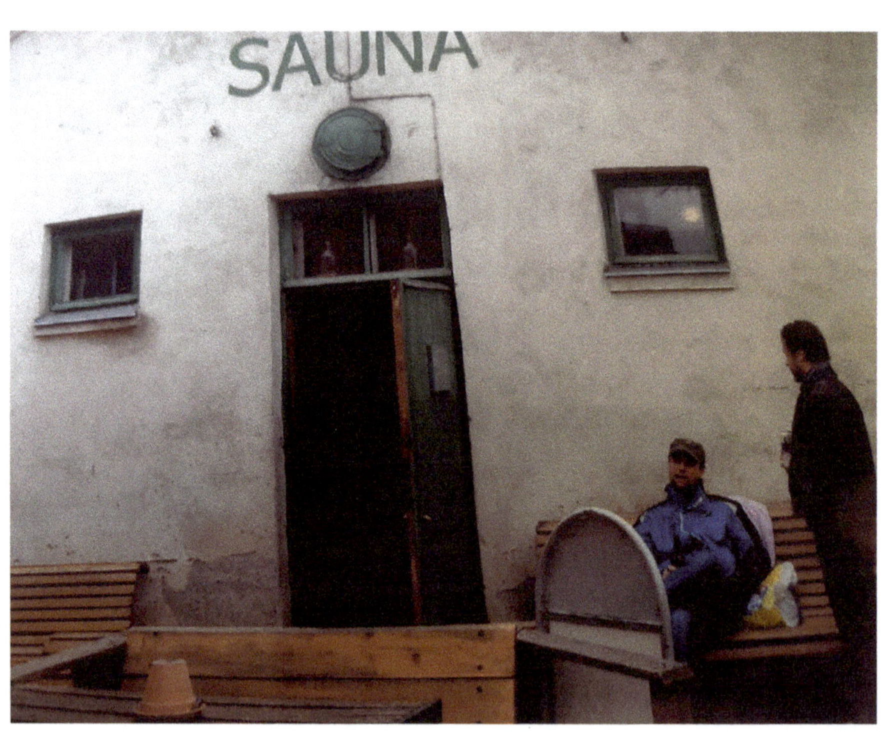
SAUNA

Prior Previous-Ness

for Jane Weiss

In the hotel sauna with Jane in Helsinki, we relax our previous-ness. Lost in sweat and shower, heated meditation, far from New York City, and our jobs teaching writing to immigrant students. We must get back. We un-do done graduate school striving, for hot-heat relaxation, nudity. Beer spigot outside this sauna, but no beer. We ride the street car, to see the *Tom of Finland* exhibit, to sit by the Gulf of Finland with its pleasure boats, listening to birds. Light gathers fierce strength throughout May. Jane returns to Suomi every two years for the Maple Leaf & Eagle conference. We drip, we pour water. Touch the wooden bench. In our prior previous-ness we were not close. Here, we glisten. Crave small crunchy *muikku* fish, fried in kettles, but it's not quite summer, not quite midnight sun.

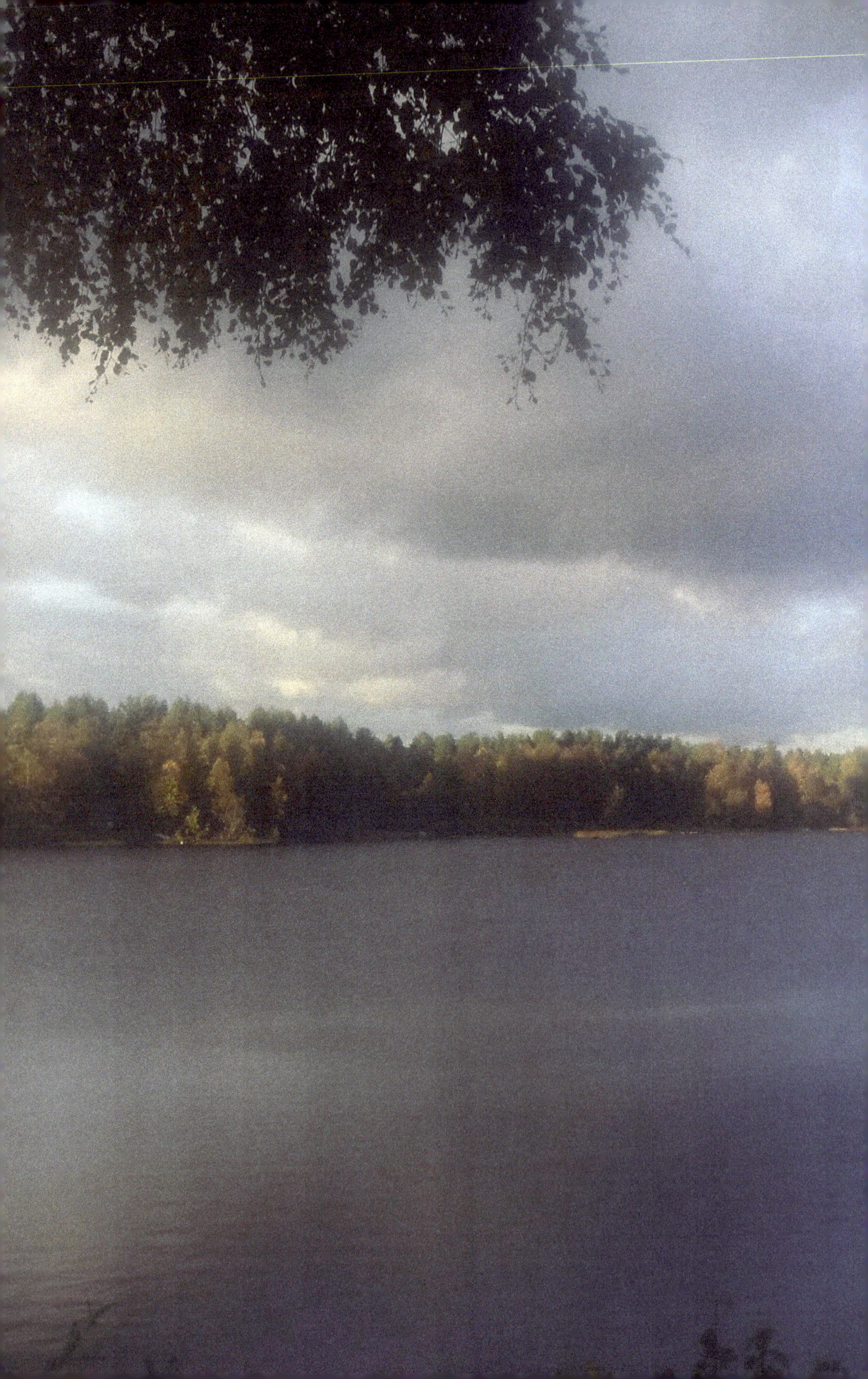

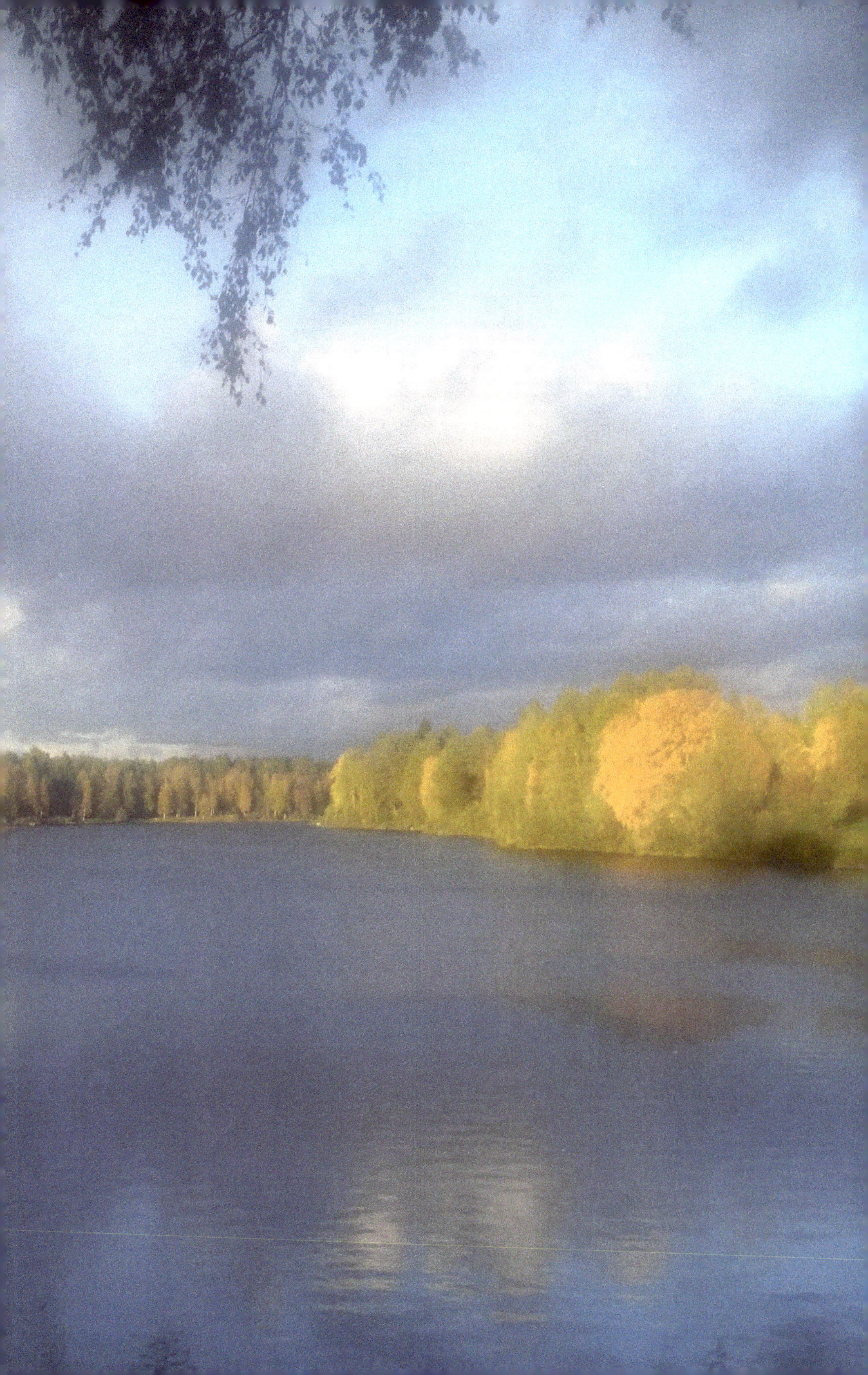

Tom's Homemade Sauna: July 4th, Conway, Massachusetts

Tom's homemade sauna, down the hill, in the Conway woods where countless wild parties and naked group photos remain from "forty years ago." They drank homemade mead. Young scions of old New England families, country squires tracing ancestry to Emily Dickinson, these pacifists refused to fight in Vietnam. They shunned careers to build cabins. He and his brother distantly civil, their compounds separated by a wooden bridge, Tom fancies himself "backhoe operator." He plows dirt, mends the path to his rustic cabin. A linguist with a penchant for travel and story-telling, Tom's self-taught in Finnish and Swedish. He studied philosophy in Germany. Now his shelves sag with detective fiction, history of genetics, old copies of *The Sun*. Tom pulls ancient grammar exercise books, photos of long-gone lovers wedged in a crumbling album. Terry, a gal who returned, introduced us.

At those parties, nudity was *de rigueur*, stones hauled by all to build a house, pond dug and filled with run-off from the creek. Now Tom must drain the swimming hole because Terry's flip-flop got stuck in muck after we waded in. Forty years ago, Tom didn't need a hearing aid to understand, or go to sleep when the sun went down. His place, sprawling and wild, his hair and beard long and white. He's put in solar panels, not hot water. Ticks have become a problem. We peel off our clothes this 4th of July in Western Massachusetts, enter Tom's homemade sauna. Heat builds in our teeth. We need the plunge-pond for muddying burning feet. We need water.

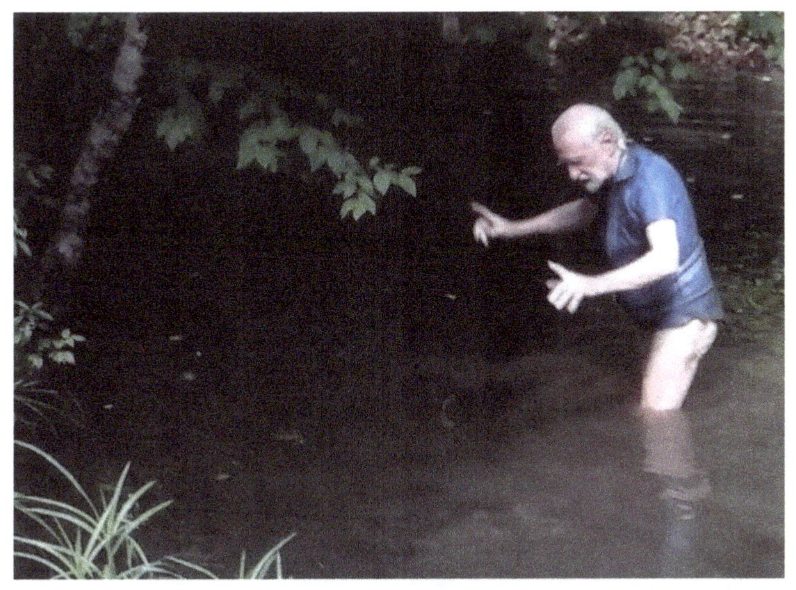

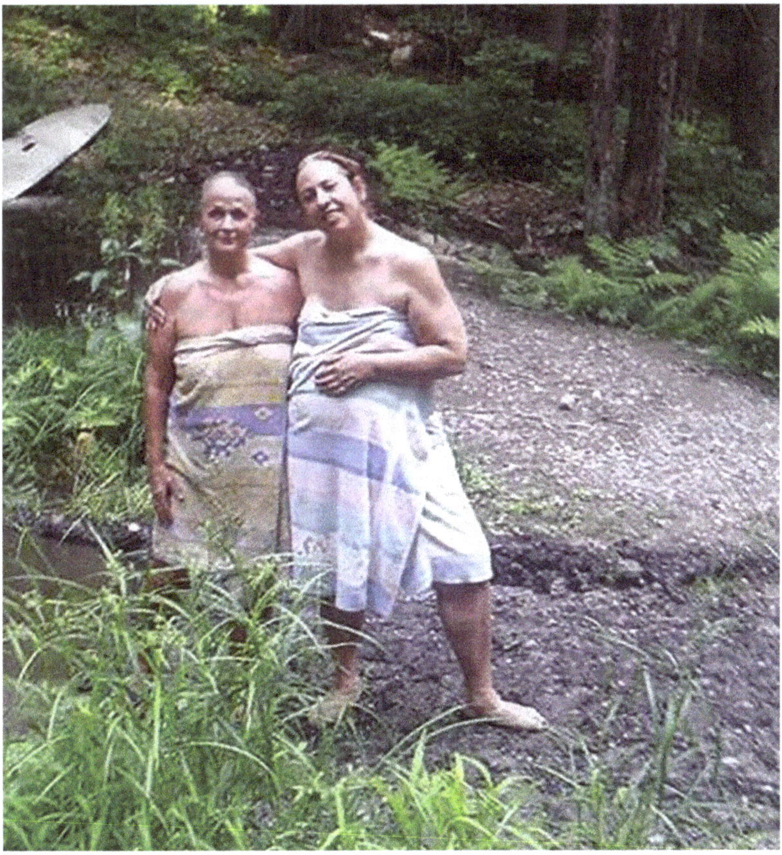

Another Round of Heat

In the sauna water rolls off *löyly*.
An older lady, a mistress of the Northland
Decides how hot, how often it hisses.
Her skin glows in orange-rind heat.
Her friend prods her. A timid guest, I am
not able to immerse in the gray ice lake.
They clean their feet in the bucket
after their plunge
naked except for paper shoes.

The sound of singing wind.
A cold May, long light.
How does that sampo in the epic produce
grain, salt and gold from thin air?

Nils-Aslak Valkeapää, Sami artist and poet
built his house on the Alta road in a sloping rock
resembling a turf hut.

He *yoiked* his song in a six-sided room.

The music
almost died out.

His journey paralleled birds
and reindeer. Spread his culture, migrating.

He preferred to stay by himself
singing in the North.
I wish you would join me
instead of keeping your distance.
Like the magpie in Helsinki watching
from the roof of a car.

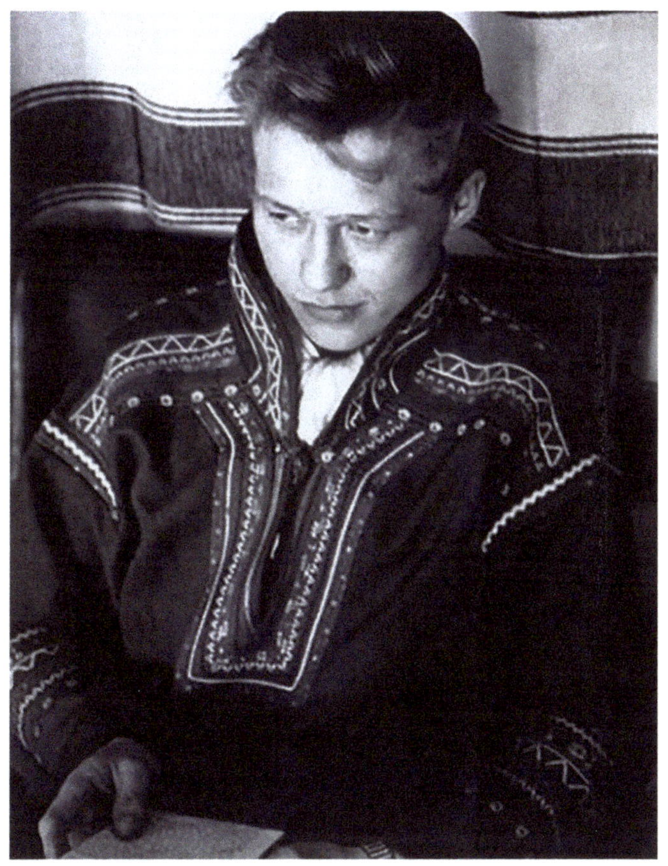

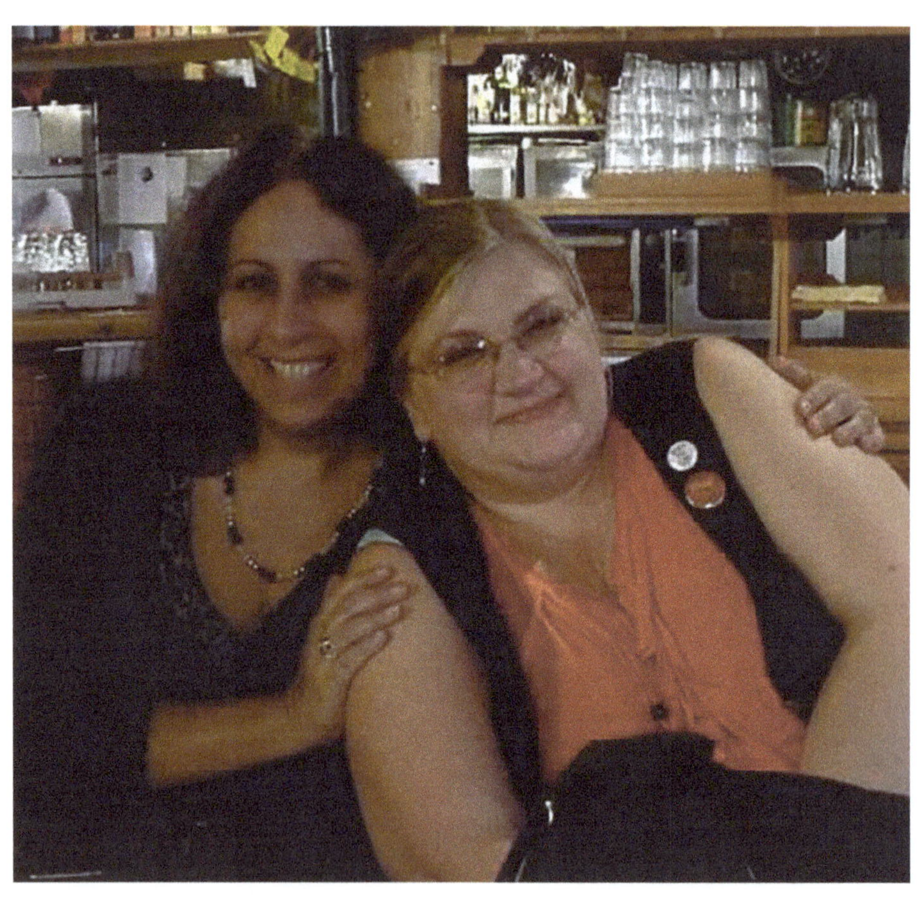

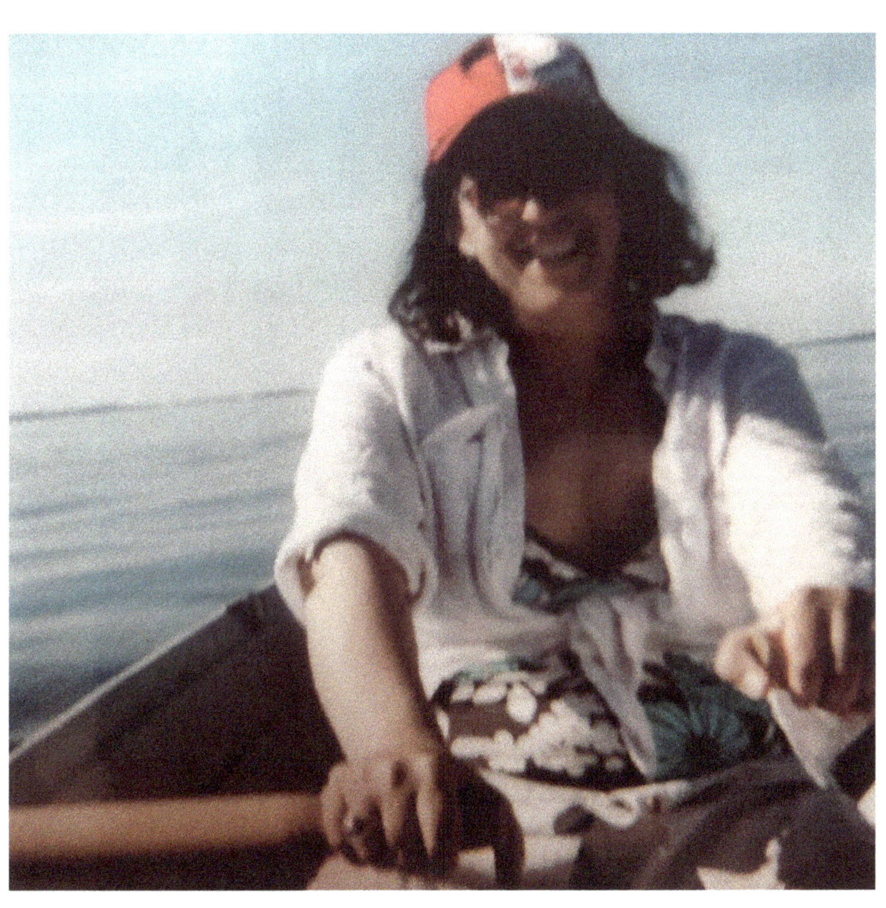

The Ice Hotel at Jukkasjärvi, Sweden

Sun glares off our sunglasses.
April above the Arctic Circle.

Sophie, Nikko and I set out to visit
The Ice Hotel
giant rectangular igloos
where tourists sleep in furs dreaming
with white candles and mirrors.

They charge high fees to enter the Ice Hotel.
We won't pay to survey beds with reindeer pelts
fantastic bird memories in glass.

Down the road the Sami cafe in a *lavvu* tent
its central fire warms us we seek the sky
through
the top of its folds.

Ice sharp yet fragile.
This town was a Sami market place.
Now murals of Sami depicted in colorful *gáktis*
with Lutheran missionaries
in the small red church dating from 1607.
I hear stones breathe.

Not far away, the colossal Kiruna iron-ore mine
bores deeper, operating 24 hours a day.

The town is sinking. Citizens, monuments, homes must
be moved or demolished
From cracks and crevices, the sound of cash.

Iron and ice
Time's refraction   water's rise.

        Sophie and Nikko hold my arms.
Guide me from step to street.
        Without any boots I'm a sliding stone.

She's a Sami filmmaker excavating
        the past as ongoing.
Every time a child climbed in the playground
        a mine hulked poisoning
        the sky. Ore always matters more.

        He's a miner like her father.
What shape, love's glint?
        Nations circle the water, on alert
        to take more.
        Ice and glaciers melt
with ease
        into the Barents Sea.

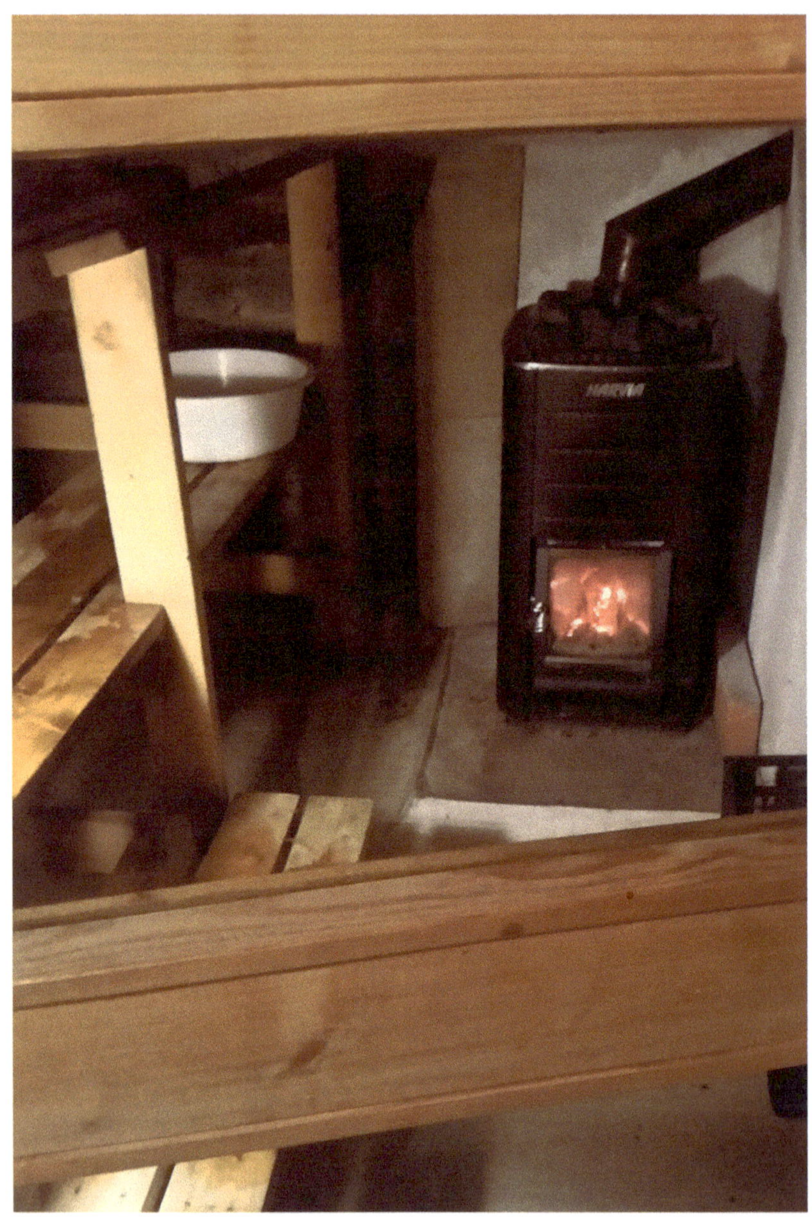

Turbulent Cruise-Ship Sauna

On a rough sea, dark with remains of Hurricane José, our ship plows through gray mist towards Halifax, Nova Scotia. Carnival's red fog horn blasts and blasts again. We reel. My friend's withered head on pillow in our cabin after she vomits in the toilet. I cut through the spa to the women's locker room, open tempered-glass door. The sauna isn't hot enough for Amy from Queens with a sinus condition, Jennie from Fort Lee, a Chinese-American who sickens when eating rice. They spread on slatted wooden benches with eucalyptus oil and towels. Jennie on top bench, knees in the air. Amy below. Bucket and ladle in the corner. I pour water on the rocks in the stove, form a cloud of steam around our eyes. Unhappy love affairs might be settled with the results of such vapors, according to Finnish myth. The Sami *lavvu* tent, set up and taken down for nomadic reindeer herding, creates comfort, central fire in a ring of rocks. Amy wants to quit her job. Jennie's just retired. What's next in these troubling times? Away from the mainland with our terrifying president, queasy inside wet waves. The Captain announces we're moving 20 nautical miles an hour, with ten-foot swells, 40 MPH winds. Canada's approaching. Oh Canada.

Yrjönkatu, Finland's Oldest Swimming Hall

This oldest public indoor swimming hall dates
        from 1928. Around the corner in Kamppi, near
Helsinki's vertebrae, we slink.

        Sessions by gender   with optional
nude swimming. Pay at the entrance. Towels cost extra.

Women old and young, of every shape   naked or not
        tingle and talk.

We take steps from steam   to smoke
        to electric.

I can't see without my glasses   in vapor clouds.

The balcony overlooks that turquoise pool with lanes.
Order a beer at one of the tables soak up the strokes.

Book a private room   between hot sessions.
        Rest on padded cots.
I take an American friend
        Who never felt so at ease.

Arched columns, cobble-stone street
Snow melting.   Pores open.

I choose to swim in the slow lane.

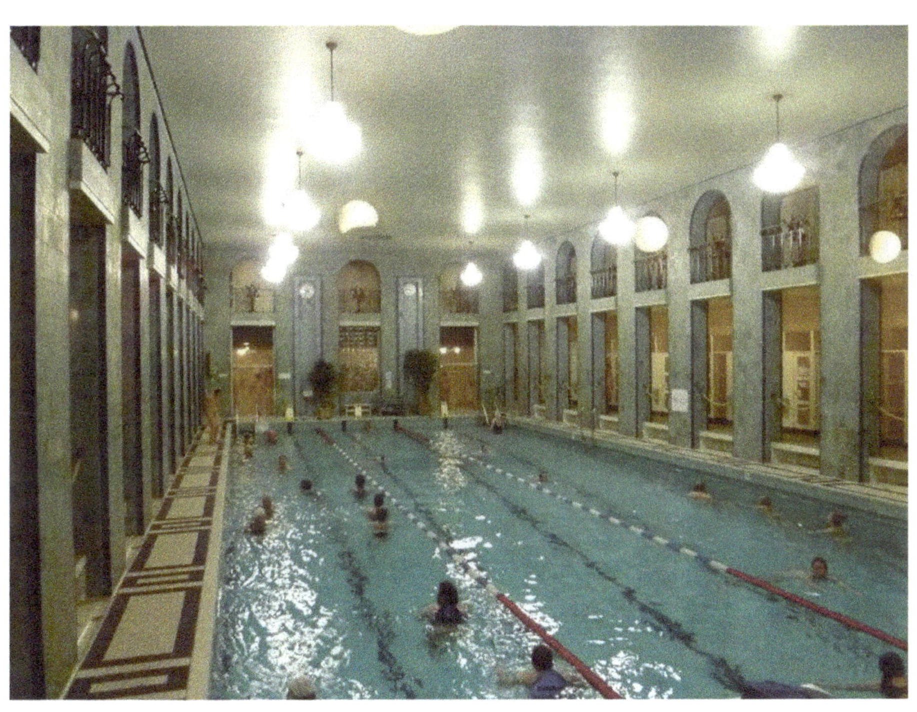

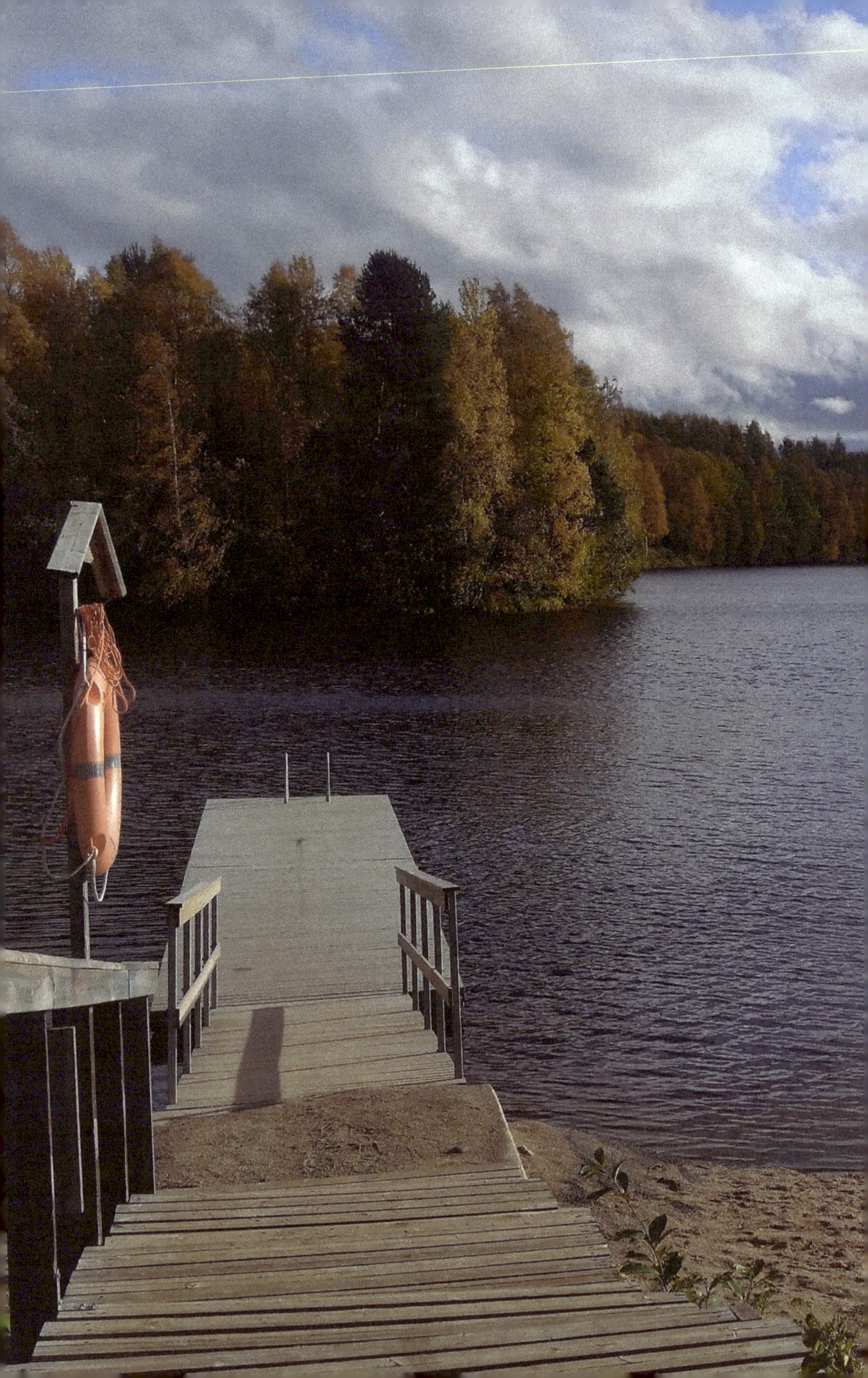

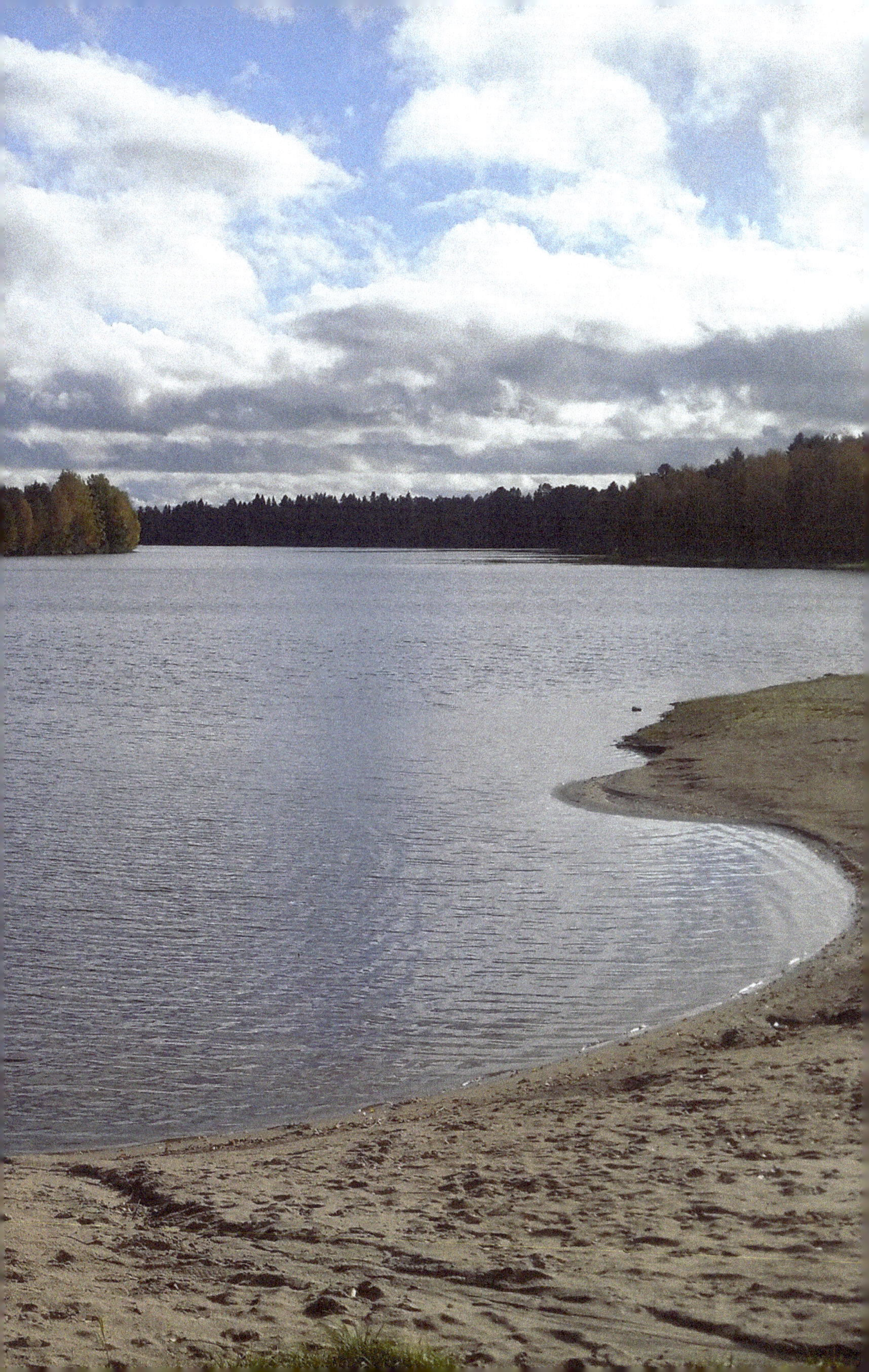

Artist's Residency at Ii

Along the Ii river, water's cold but I swim
anyway.   Early September
row boats waiting, shy.

Sami artist Carola Grahn carved these words
on a sign along the river: "My Name is Nature
Please Fuck Me."

Sanna, sculptor of bronze, founder of this
            residency lives next door.
She shows me where to pick
lingonberries, bilberries, tart and small
everywhere on low vines.

In the center of Ii pronounced "Eeeeee,"
the young man behind the counter at Orient Kebob/Pizza
Tells us in perfect Finnish he's an Iraqi Kurd. One of only
a few in a small Finnish town. His family was gassed
during the war with Iran.   Ii is said to be a modification
of a Sami word
For place to stay overnight.
I stay for a month in the Northland
To make bridges with words
air-girl
water-daughter
city-dweller-in-the mushroom forest.
Sanna invites me to eat with them
at the table in her yard.
"I have worked all alone for many years,"
she exclaims, serving salmon, potatoes and salad.
Her old friend B. whom she met when her
husband abandoned her, is full of the drink.

He calls me stupid in between his rapid sneezes.
He assumes I voted for Trump
and I cannot convince him
otherwise.

Sanna sculpts women in leaves, women with fish,
Graffitied women, women with feathers, women in treetops.
Their faces shine.
She offers rides to her friend also named Sanna
who doesn't own a car but
drives a taxi at night.
Survival is our name. Don't fuck with us.

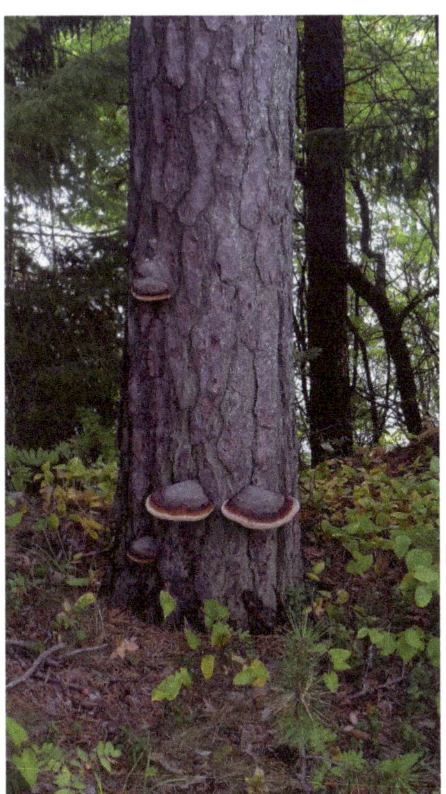

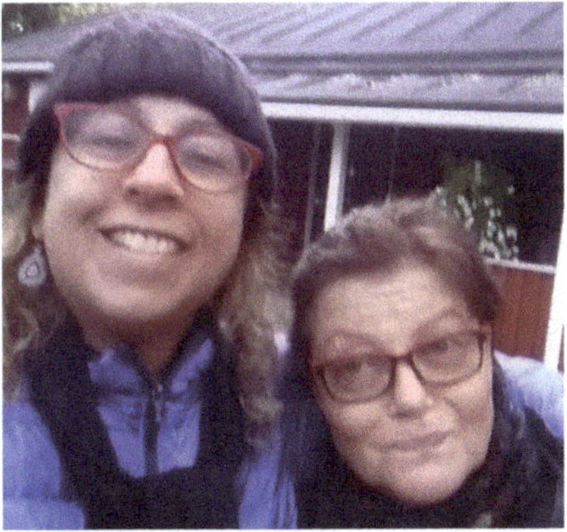

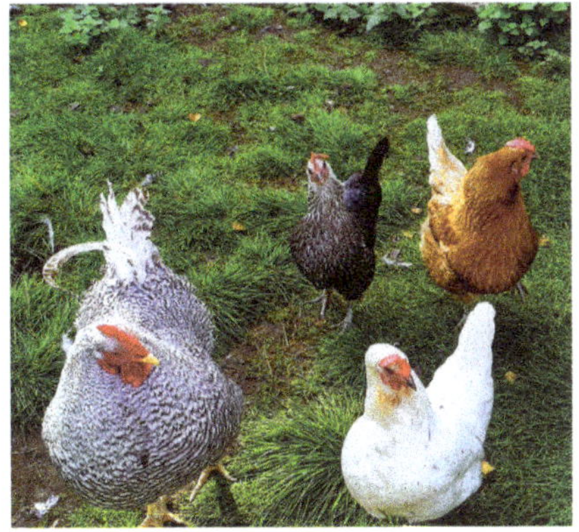

"The oak skillfully answered: Indeed there is wood in me for one small boat's hull." The *Kalevala*, 16: 77–80

Father & Son in Row Boat

The father rows, oars up and over the shell. Certainty of a river's current heading home from island Illinsaari. The 20-something son's tangled hair in his face, not quite dreadlocks. He rolls his own cigarettes and smells of them. He leans towards the setting sun, blue-black water against pine and birch. The father's smile eclipses scant-spoken English; the son repeats my name. "You look Israeli," he says, full of mischief, slouching, high or drunk.

His Finnish father rows as the sun falls away; his mother remains in Stuttgart. How do these angular men pass each day on their island of berry stalks and *herkkutatti* mushrooms spouting after rain? What do they discuss? They understand I long to ride in a small boat on the rushing river, oars in current, transported between moon and shore. We met at a gathering. Now they row me to the artist's residence. After they drop me at the dock, I watch them cut to their island, silhouettes in moon rise. I shall return for more strokes. When light appears, when boats clang against docks holding flower pots. I'll meet them someday at half tide.

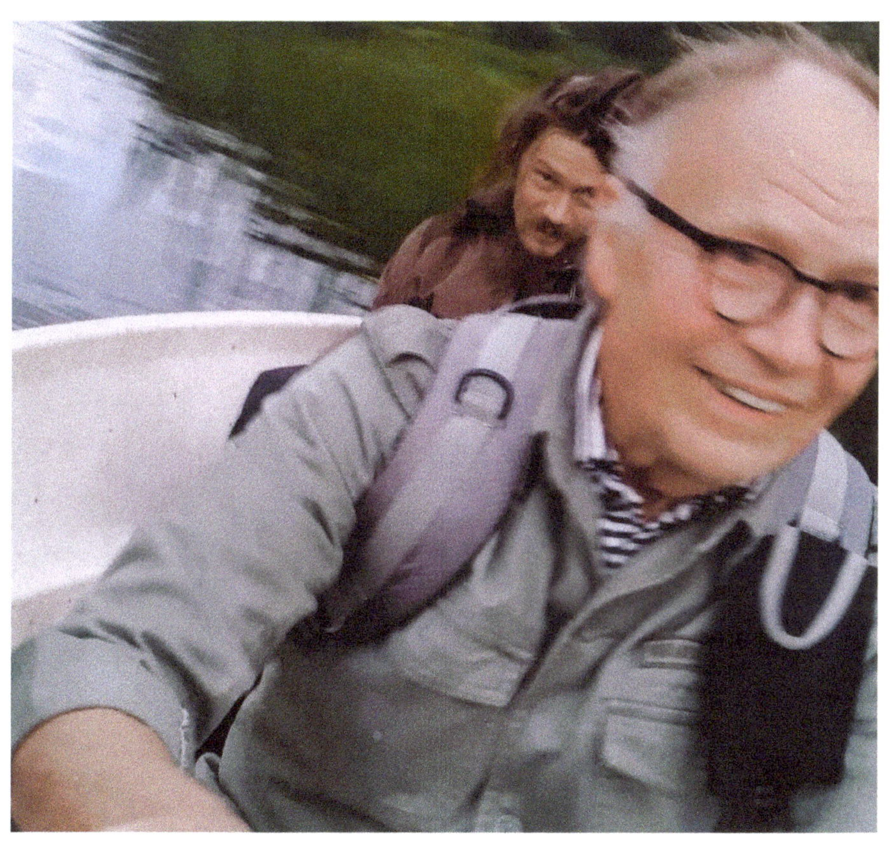

"The mistress lives well: she slices up buns, stuffs herself with pies, spreads butter on them." The *Kalevala* 33: 25–28

Live Simply

1. Dave's Housewarming

After I eat Lea's green nettle-potato bread, her seed bread, her fruit loaf, drink her home-made wine, admire the sweater she knitted for her daughter, we dance at Dave's housewarming party. Dave swapped England for Finland, Brexit burnt toast in his throat. The improvisers turn up their computerized trance music, a keyboard is struck with a toothbrush and sex toy for vibration while we shake. Noako from Japan pressed a print of fern into a card, wrote my name in Japanese characters. She swallows salmon soup with gratitude. After the Fukushima nuclear accident, they test vegetables for radioactivity.

2. Lea and Leon's Home

Lea and Leon invite me to their home, down a dirt road in the direction of Kemi. He makes sailboats from wood, practices his craft, can't hear in one ear. Might he sing like old Väinämöinen in the *Kalevala* as he chops wood and considers the origin of words? Photos on the wall display every hull he's forged. Lea knits socks and mittens, pink and gray, purple, red, thick for cold months filling up shelves. She sews clothes for a baby doll dressed like a child of the North. Her workroom holds four sewing machines with various needles. "We live simply," she says, "we don't need much." I call her Martha Stewart of northern Ostrobothnia, but she's never heard of Martha.

3. Ali's Room

Ali from Afghanistan lives upstairs. He grew up dreaming of Nokia, gadgets, magic screens. When his parents died during the war, he walked to this country of reindeer and boreal forest, learned to speak Finnish. At first, he helped Leon build boats, but now he earns more at the nuclear plant being built with Putin. He maintains machinery, operates gauges, troubleshoots. His axe hangs in Leon's toolshed. Lea's socks line his boots.

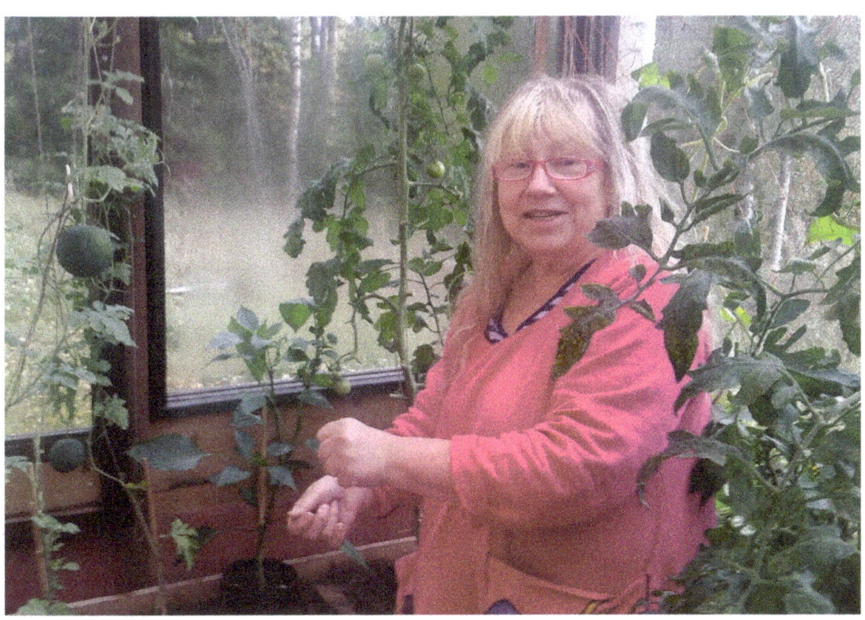

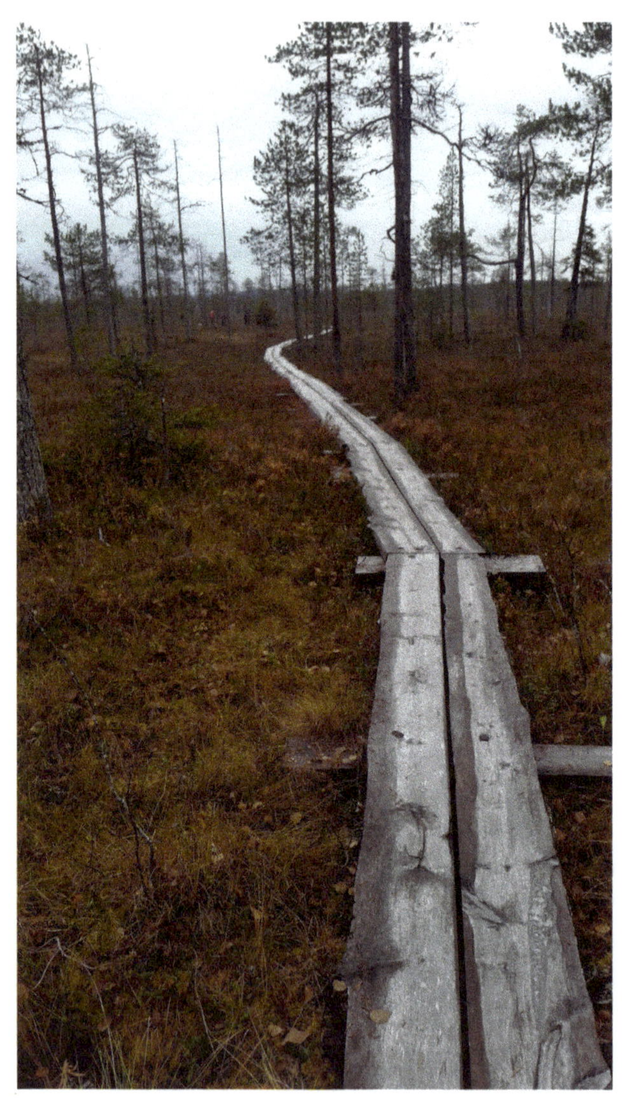

Origin & Motion

In the *Kalevala*, a barren water-mother's knee is the place

where birds lay eggs. The bottom half of a smashed egg becomes

earth. In Sami myth, the Sun goddess is the mother of humankind.

My mother, a widow, grows old in a hot place.

She wants to stay put while I alight in foreign lands.

The sound of a yodel emerges from one's chest and throat; the

Sami *yoiks* a longing

in the heart. My mother's voice cuts through woods like the earth

in dark rye bread. Motion molds us into elements

beyond our drives. My mother worries in syllables she cannot sing.

Pain arrives in her feet like eggs hatched.

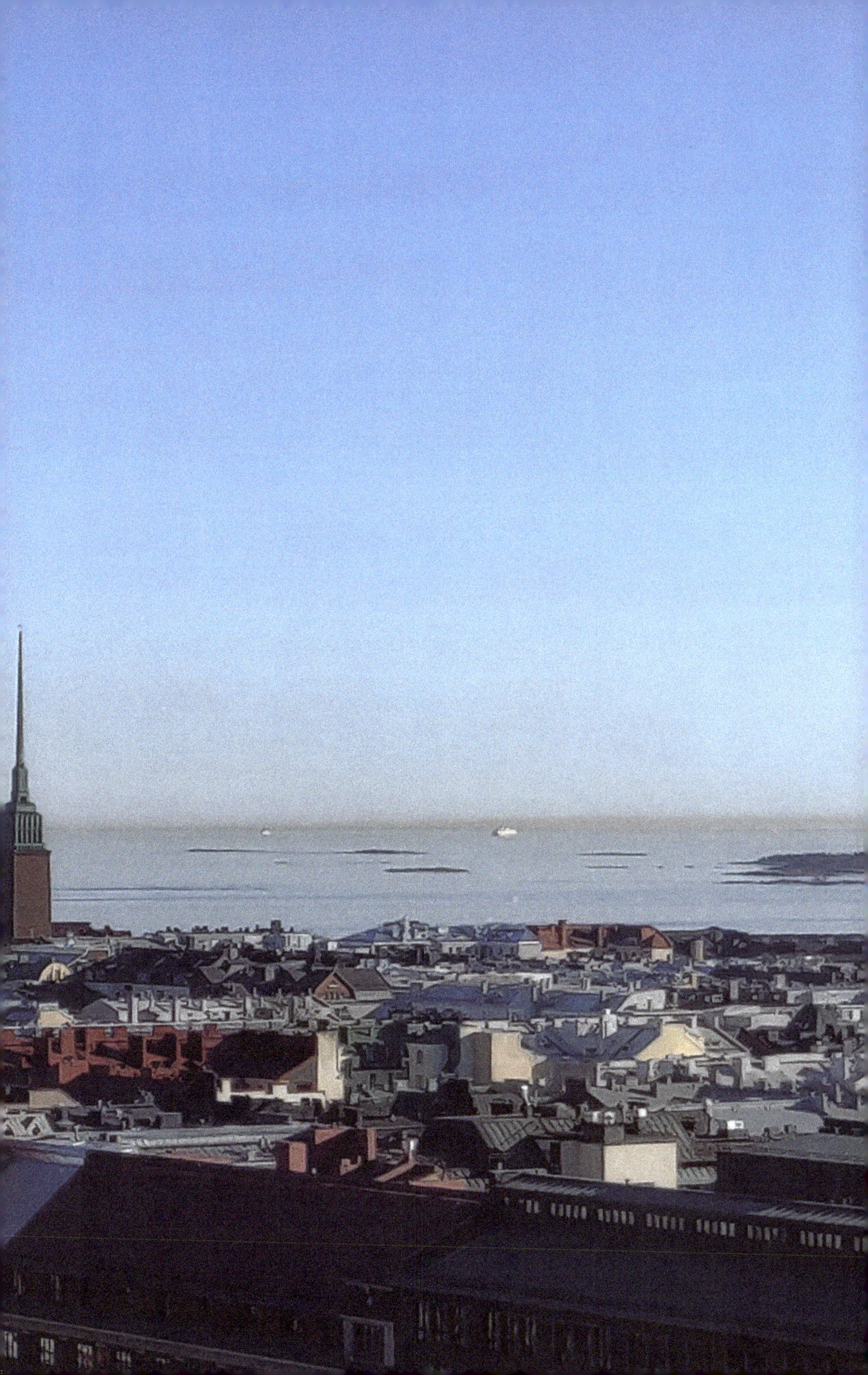

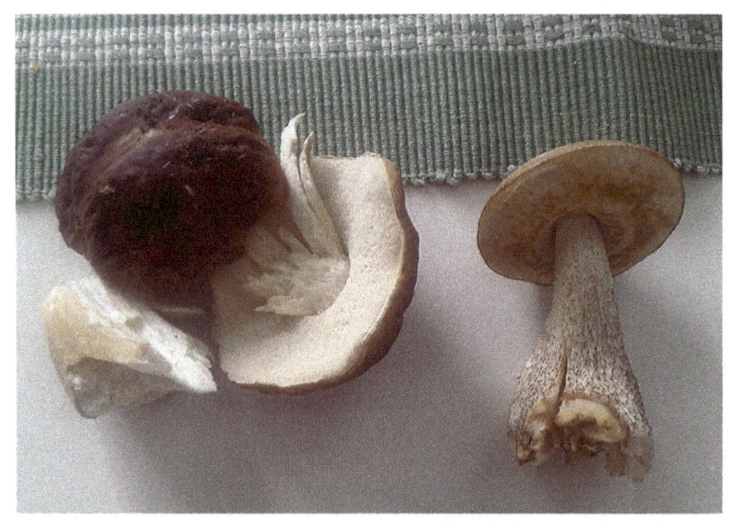

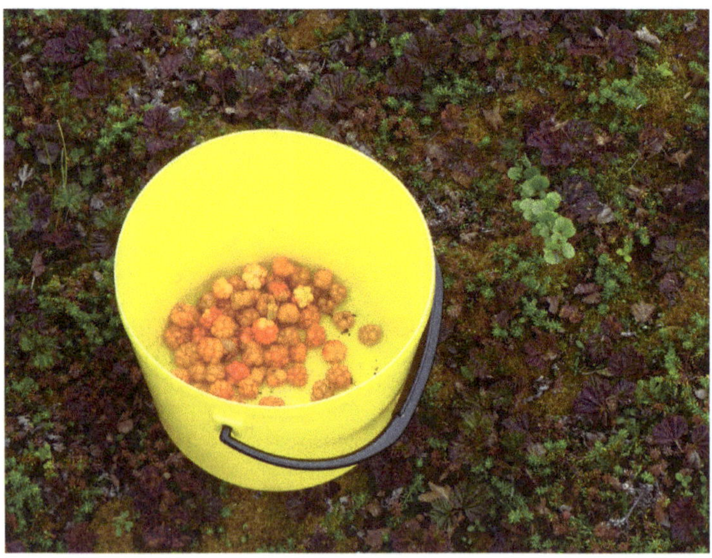

Foraging

With Antti in the woods   I learn to spot
herkkutatti aka *boletus edulis*   aka porcini mushrooms.
Large brown caps   tubes extending from
underside. In Italian folklore, they sprout
at the new moon. Sauté them, for a slightly nutty meaty fruity
flavor. The small ones, maggot-free. Once I understand
where and when they may appear even late in the season, I am
hooked.
            It takes patience, a good eye.

With Lena and Kaisa, I'm eager to pick yellow cloudberries   in bogs.
            We put on high boots   carry buckets   to find them.
Glamourous, rare   in a mosquito haze   in the Swedish Sami area
            not far from Kiruna. *Rubus chamaemorus*, grown in
                        wild alpine, arctic tundra, boreal forest.
                        "Everyman's land"
            means Norwegians   can drive over, grab a prime spot
                        and they do.
            Finns make Lakka liquor from these yellow berries.
The soft, juicy fleshy berry garners high prices   in markets.
            Kaisa's mother Anna   prepares jam and pancakes from the
contents of   their nearly-full buckets. They serve me from this
bounty   even though
                        I did not pull my weight.

Hailuoto Island

On the mainland, I broke a glass in a cafe.
On the island I climbed a spiral staircase, slept on a low bed.
On the mainland, I watched the dreadful Brett Kavanaugh confirmation
        hearings on my phone.
On the island, Silja loaded the stove with wood for sauna.
We waited until it was hot enough writing totems to the forest.

Consider motion and stasis, a series of curves.
The world endures construction of malls and towers
ordinal and cardinal. Forests from islands become logs piled high
near train stations. Bound for China.

Complex harmonic circles
Radius and line. Geological time
outruns us.

The ferry to the island held our bus.
The driver serves as the island's mailman.
The island grows like tiny moths you rarely see.
Someday, it shall attach to the mainland.

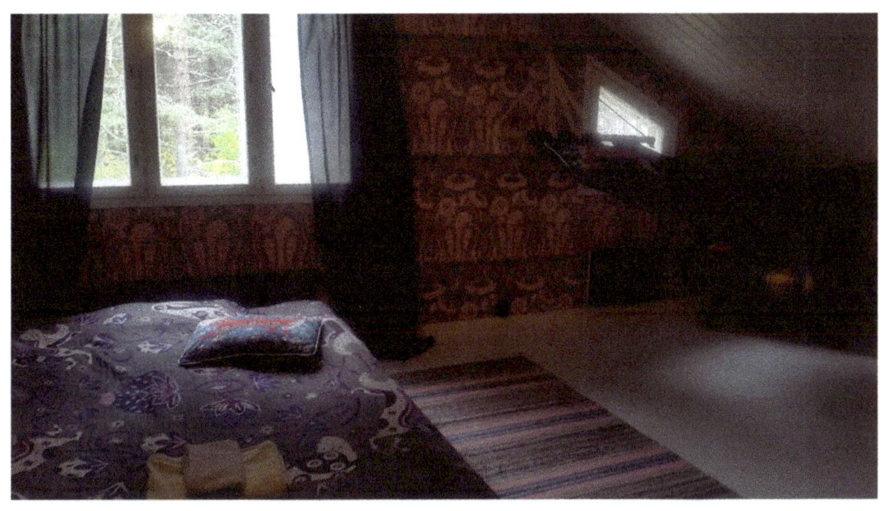

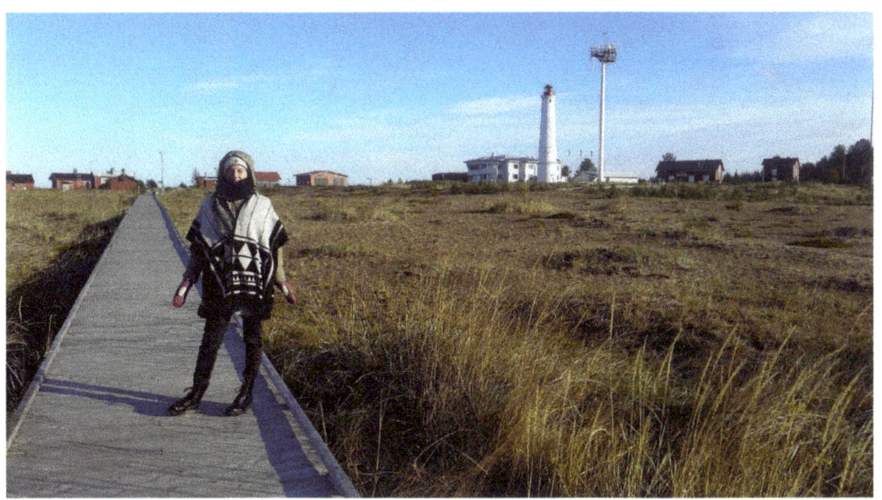

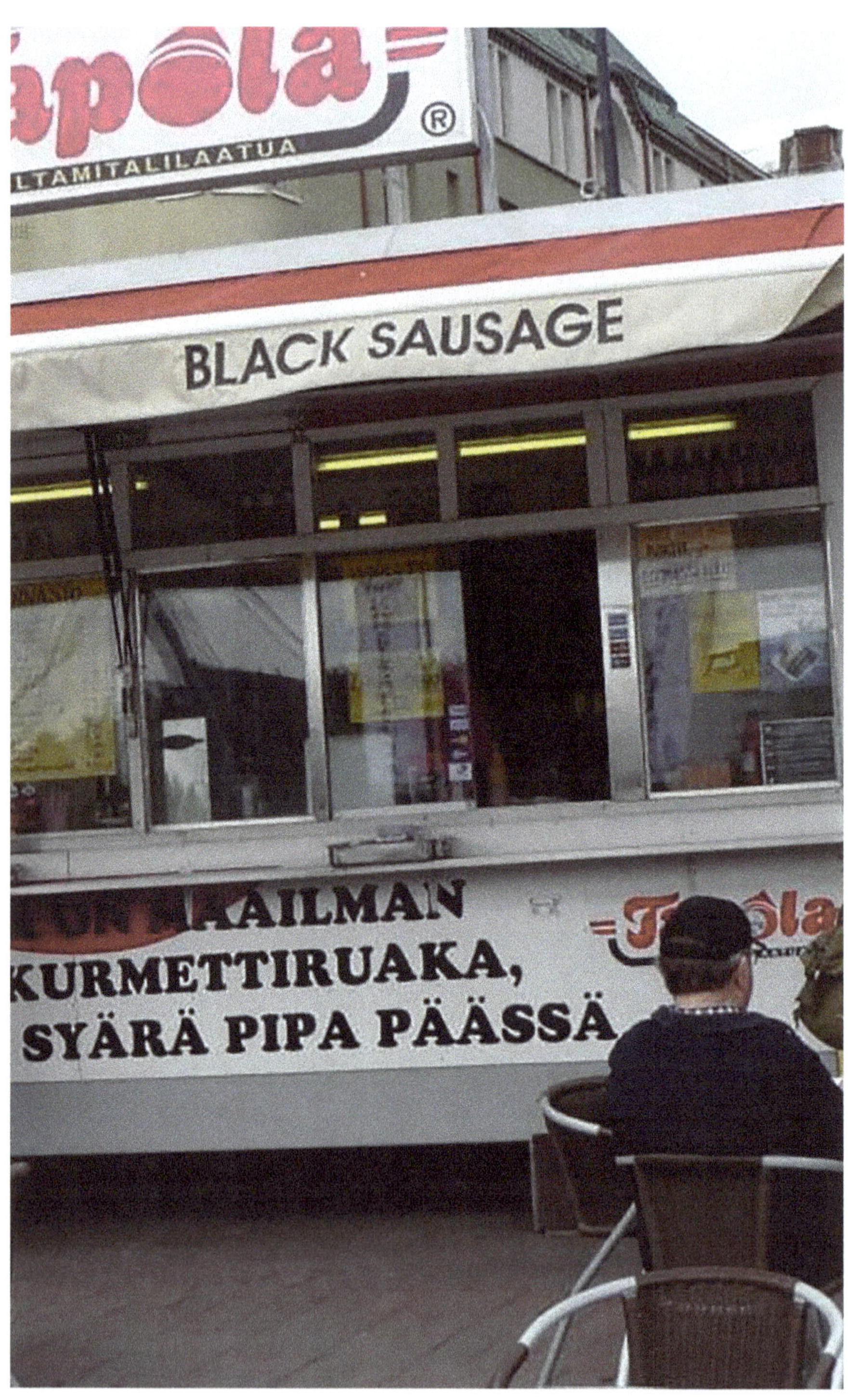
BLACK SAUSAGE
KURMETTIRUAKA,
SYÄRÄ PIPA PÄÄSSÄ

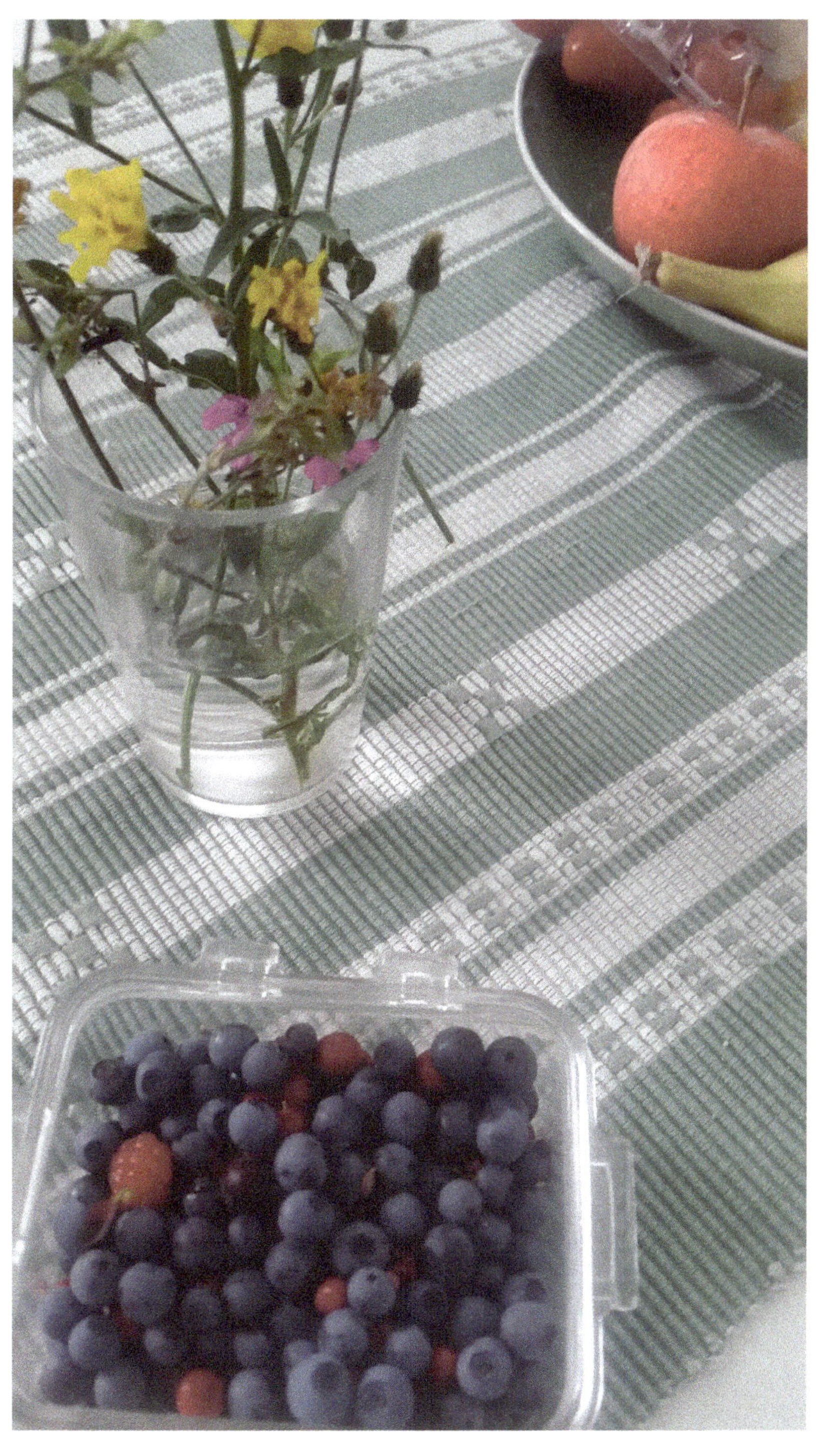

Unreliable Snowpack

In the *Kalevala*,
birds lay eggs
in a barren water-mother's knee.

The bottom half of a smashed egg becomes
earth. In Sami myth, the sun goddess
is the mother of humankind.

In winter, our experiment includes flooding an icicle.
Something went wrong in the undergrowth.
Reindeer can't forage for lichen
trapped between layers
rain-on-snow.
Melt, freeze, melt, freeze.
Death follows.

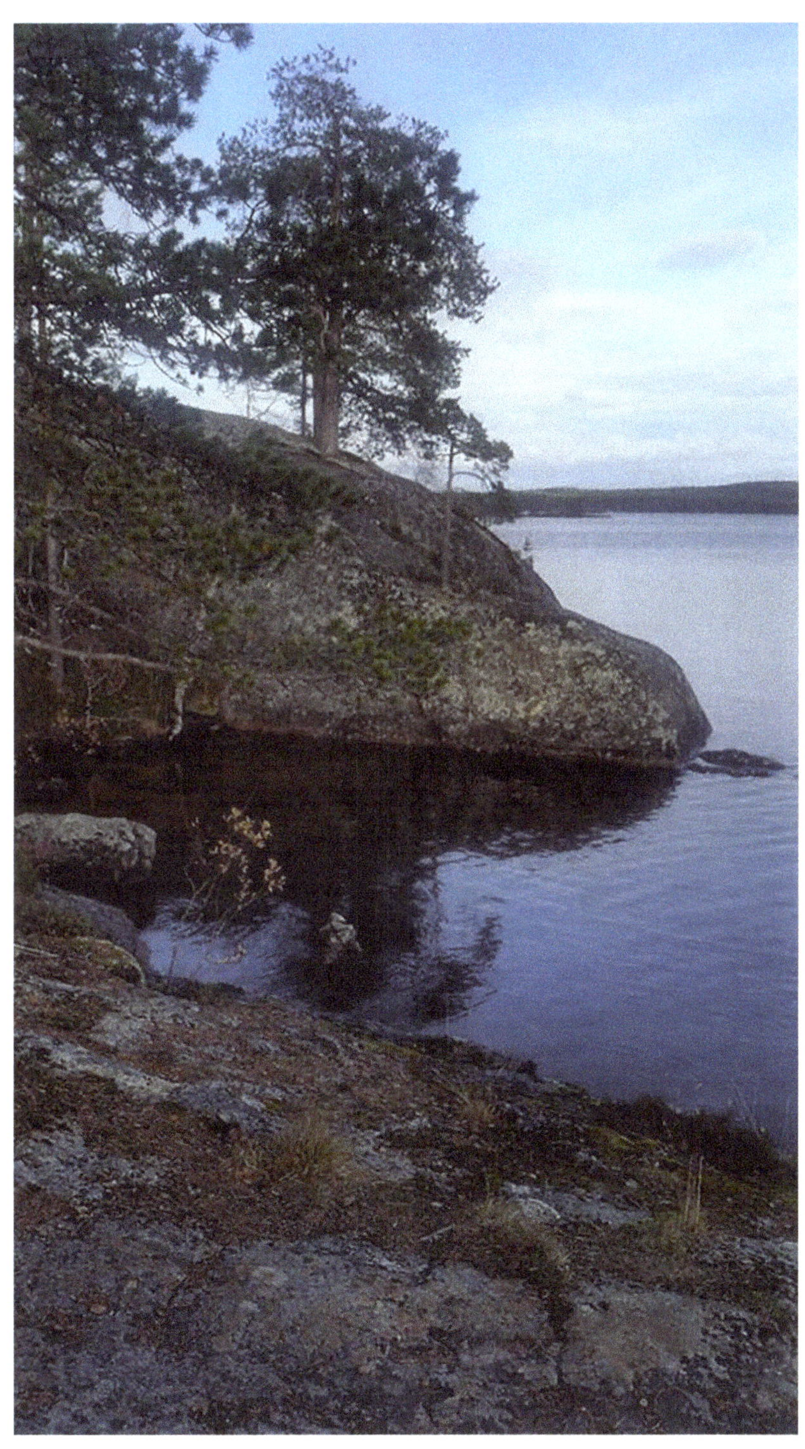

Unsuspecting Believers

Pilgrims crossed the second curved bridge.
Liars cross the line so often they fell bridges.
A van drove into turbulent seas filled with unsuspecting believers.

Can you experience pure goodness, envying others as you do?
Living with the senseless demagogue who orders more bridges when there's no longer a river?

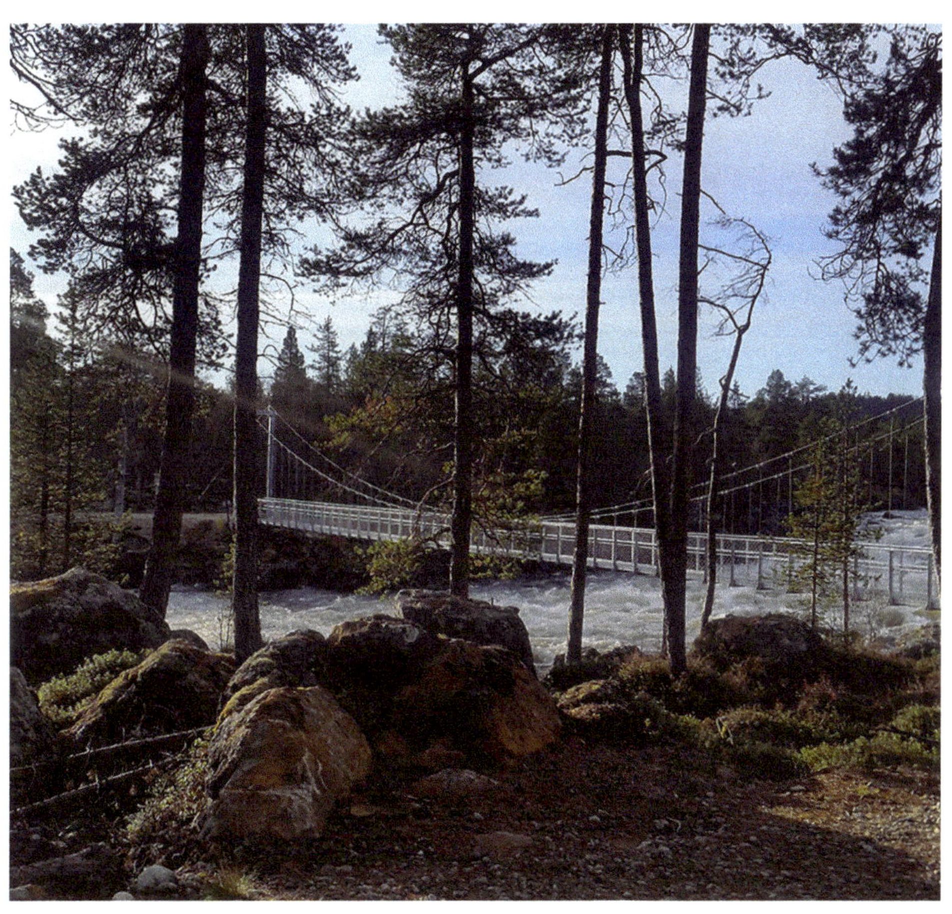

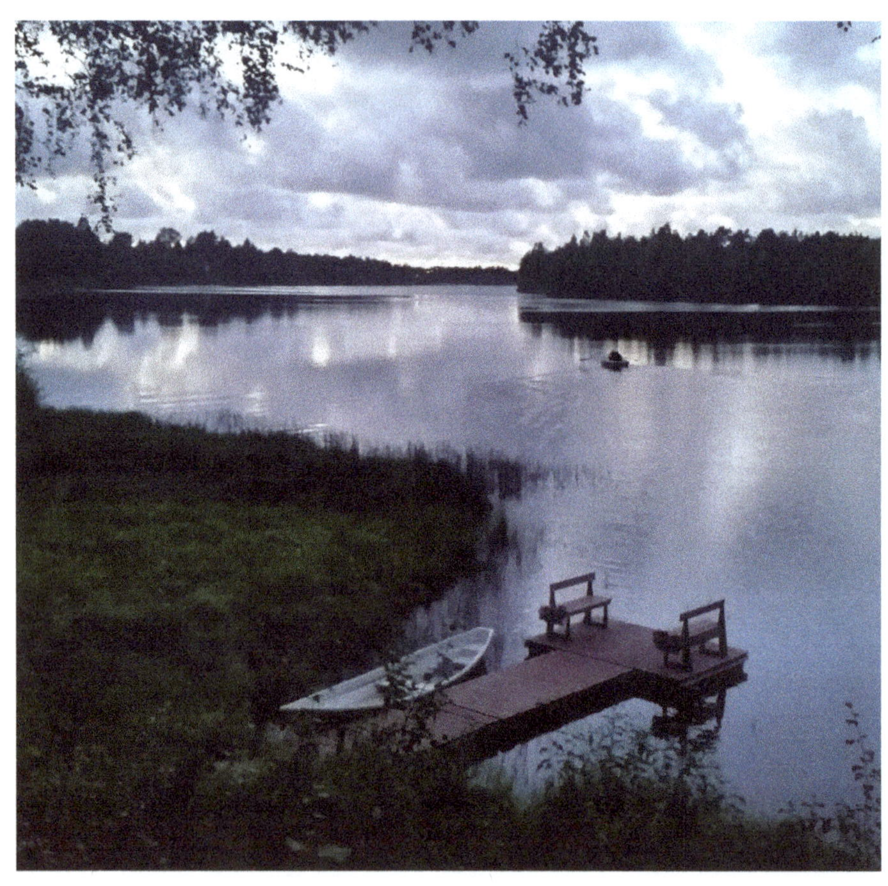

Two Maids in Töölö Towers Sauna

Annika arrives at the small sauna in Töölö Towers.

Heat rises like tolerance. Our friendship expands and quiets
over eleven years since I first visited Suomi. We eat and drink
and shop and walk.

Two maids sharing a view of Helsinki from the 11th floor deck.
Taking non-traditional paths, content with in-betweens.
How pleasant for me to flit here.

We pour water on the rocks, over nakedness. Leave
imperfection
          and judgment.
Sweat and cold, wood and skin. The time of dry smoke. Music
          collective and separate.

Annika collects lamps of artificial light that shine in the
darkness of her living room. Omnipresent candles in the night.

She visits her aging father in their cottage near the archipelago
where Russians purchase islands. I lost my father this year. He
slipped out of the room.

The Gulf of Finland edges against moonlight, tumescent water
resembling a lake.

The happy and the lucky by the headlands. Longing for eternal things.

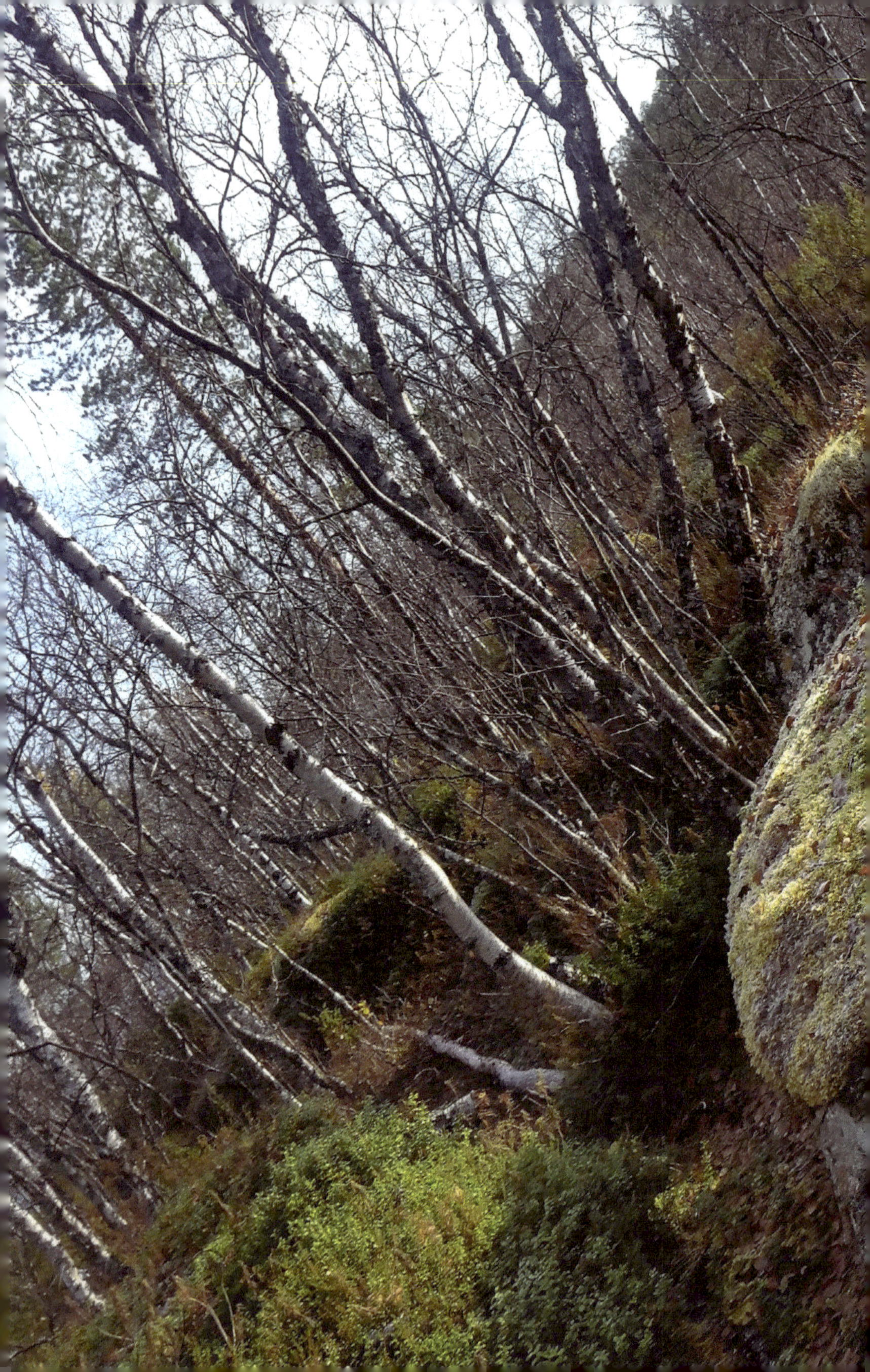

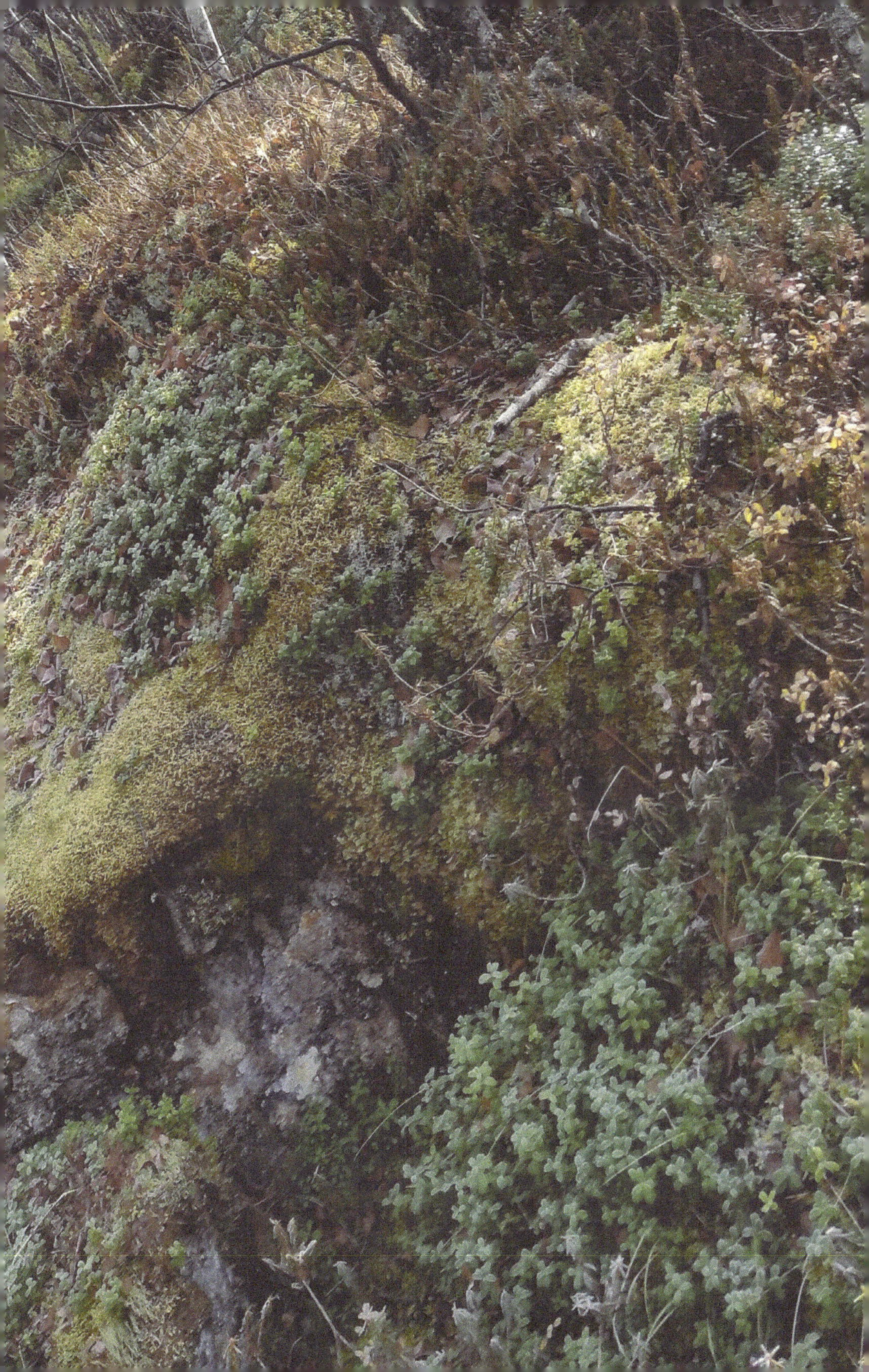

Notes on Images

All photos in this book, unless otherwise noted, are by Cheryl J. Fish.

[Cover] The cover image, titled *A Finlandish Bath*, is taken from *Travels through Sweden, Finland, and Lapland, to the North Cape, in the years 1798 and 1799*, by Joseph Acerbi. The image itself is a wood engraving with watercolor, by Olof Sörling. The book contains the following information about what is happening in the image:

Almost all the Finnish peasants have a small house built on purpose for a bath: it consists of only one small chamber, in the innermost part of which are placed a number of stones, which are heated by fire till they become red. On these stones, thus heated, water is thrown, until the company within be involved in a thick cloud of vapour. In this innermost part, the chamber is formed into two stories for the accommodation of a greater number of persons within that small compass; and it being the nature of heat and vapour to ascend, the second story is, of course, the hottest. Men and women use the bath promiscuously, without any concealment of dress, or being in the least influenced by any emotions of attachment . . .

The Finlanders, all the while they are in this hot bath, continue to rub themselves, and lash every part of their bodies with switches formed of twigs of the birch-tree. In ten minutes they become as red as raw flesh, and have altogether a very frightful appearance. In the winter season they frequently go out of the bath, naked as they are, to roll themselves in the snow . . . which is the same thing as going out of boiling into freezing water! . . . By the bath, they tell you, their strength is recruited as much as by rest and sleep.

[Fpc] This image of a sauna is extracted from page 90 of volume 1 of *Finland I Nordiska Museet*, by Artur Immanue Hazelius.

[16] Photograph of the Gulf of Finland by Alexey Komarov, 2014. Wikimedia Commons. Creative Commons Attribution 3.0.

[19] The author's son, Josh, holding a Finnish flag.

[21] Kuusijärvi Sauna, before and during the fire depicted in the poem.

[24] Rajaportti Sauna, the oldest public sauna in the Pispala neighborhood of Tampere. Tampere was named "Sauna Capital" in 2018, as it is home to the most saunas in Finland.

[26–7] Autumn foliage, known as *ruska*, along the Iijoki River, Ii, Northern Ostrobothnia.

[29] (top) Photo by Terry Carter. Tom Manwell cools off in his pond. (bottom) Terry Carter and the author, post-sauna, Conway, Massachusetts

[31] Nils-Aslak Valkeapää (1943–2001), Sami writer, musician, and artist. Photograph taken sometime between 1962 and 1965. The author visited his house in Skibotn, Norway, in 2011. Wikimedia Commons.

[32] The author with Angie Pohja in Telakka Bar and Restaurant, Tampere.

[33] The author rowing on Lake Näsijärvi.

[40–1] Empty autumn beach on Iijoki River, near the artist's residency in Ii.

[43] The author with artist Sanna Koivisto and Sanna's chickens.

[47] Lea Backman in her greenhouse.

[48] Boardwalk, Aapa Mire, Pyha-Luosto National Park, near Sodankylä.

[50–1] Helsinki, facing the Gulf of Finland.

[52] Some of the author's foraged mushrooms and cloudberries.

[55] (top) The author's room at the Kulttuuritalo Päiväkoti residence. (bottom) Director Sanna Roukala with Hailuoto Island lighthouse in background.

[59] Lake Inari.

[61] Juutuanjoki River, home river of the Inari Sami people. The author walked the Juutua Nature Trail with Marjorie Shaffer in October 2018.

[64–5] Autumn woods in Ii, near the artist's residence.

Cheryl J. Fish is a poet, fiction writer, and environmental justice scholar. She is the author of *CRATER & TOWER*, poems that examine the eruption of the Mount St. Helens volcano through the lens of the terrorist attack on the World Trade Center on 9/11/01. She is the author of the chapbooks *Make It Funny, Make it Last* (#171, Belladonna) and *My City Flies By*. Her poems have appeared in *Poetics-for-the-More-than-Human World, New American Writing, Hanging Loose, Terrain.org* and elsewhere. Her short stories have been published in *Iron Horse Literary Review, CheapPopLit, Spank the Carp*, and *Liars League NYC.* Her debut novel, *OFF THE YOGA MAT*, is forthcoming from Livingston Press in 2022. Fish has written about extraction and mining in Sami areas of Fennoscandia, and Sami responses through activist film, photography, and ecomedia in publications such as *Critical Norths: Space Nature, Theory; Nordic Narratives of Nature and Environment*; and *The Journal of Scandinavian Cinema*. Fish is the author of *Black and White Women's Travel Narratives* and co-editor with Farah J. Griffin, of *A Stranger in the Village: Two Centuries of African American Travel Writing*. She has been Fulbright professor in Finland and is currently professor of English at Borough of Manhattan Community College, City University of New York, and docent lecturer in the Department of Cultures, at the University of Helsinki.

Shanti Arts

Nature ▪ Art ▪ Spirit

Please visit us online
to browse our entire book catalog,
including poetry collections and fiction,
books on travel, nature, healing, art,
photography, and more.

Also take a look at our highly
regarded art and literary journal,
Still Point Arts Quarterly, which
may be downloaded for free.

www.shantiarts.com

www.ingramcontent.com/pod-product-compliance
Lightning Source LLC
LaVergne TN
LVHW052356100826
845147LV00013B/856

* 9 7 8 1 9 5 1 6 5 1 7 4 9 *